VISUAL QUICKSTART GUIDE

THE DOJO TOOLKIT

Steven Holzner

Peachpit Press

Visual QuickStart Guide

The Dojo Toolkit
Steven Holzner

Peachpit Press
1249 Eighth Street
Berkeley, CA 94710
10/524-2178
0/524-2221 (fax)

d us on the Web at: www.peachpit.com
eport errors, please send a note to: errata@peachpit.com
pit Press is a division of Pearson Education.

Judy Ziajka
on Coordinator: Myrna Vladic
or: Christi Payne
er: Liz Welch
lie Bess
n: Peachpit Press

ights

lity

ates of America

Dedication

To Nancy, of course!

Acknowledgments

I'd particularly like to thank Wendy Sharp and Judy Ziajka for their tireless efforts to make this book the best it can be.

TABLE OF CONTENTS

	Introduction	viii
Chapter 1:	**Essential Dojo**	**1**
	About Dojo	2
	Getting Dojo	3
	Using AOL CDN to Get Dojo	5
	Getting Started with Dojo	6
	Creating a Dojo Web Page	7
	Using the Dojo Styles	8
	Preparing to Use Dijits	10
	Adding a Button Dijit	11
	Adding a TextBox Dijit	12
	Responding to Dijit Events	13
	Displaying Text in a Text Box After a Button Click	14
	Running textbox.html	16
Chapter 2:	**Form Dijits: Text Boxes and Buttons**	**17**
	Creating Dijits in Code	18
	Connecting Code to Dijits Using <script> Elements	20
	Submitting to Web Sites	22
	Debugging Dojo	24
	Using ValidationTextBox	26
	Using NumberTextBox	28
	Using DateTextBox	30
	Using TimeTextBox	32
	Using NumberSpinner	34
Chapter 3:	**Form Dijits: Combo Boxes, Toggles, and More**	**37**
	Using CheckBox	38
	Using RadioButton	40
	Using ComboBox	42
	Using ToggleButton	44
	Using MultiSelect	46
	Using Slider	48
	Using DropDownButton	50
	Using ComboButton	52

Chapter 4: **Layout Dijits** **55**

Using ContentPane 56

Adding Dijits to a Content Pane. 58

Using BorderContainer 60

Creating BorderContainer Dijits in Code 62

Using StackContainer. 64

Creating StackContainer Dijits in Code. 66

Using TabContainer. 68

Creating a TabContainer Dijit in Code. 70

Using AccordionContainer. 72

Chapter 5: **Application Dijits: Tool Tips**
and More **75**

Using Tooltip 76

Using Tooltip with Images 78

Using Dialog. 80

Using Dialog with Input. 82

Using ProgressBar 84

Using ColorPalette 86

Using ColorPalette with Dialog. 88

Using Toolbar. 90

Adding Images to Toolbar Buttons 92

Chapter 6: **Application Dijits: Menus, Trees,**
and More **95**

Using Menu. 96

Creating Context Menus 98

Creating Pop-Up Menus. 100

Creating Traditional Menus 102

Adding Menu Separators 104

Using TitlePane. 106

Using InlineEditBox. 108

Creating Tree Data. 110

Using Tree 112

Chapter 7: **Dragging and Dropping** **115**

Creating a Moveable 116

Creating Moveables in Code. 118

Adding Dijits to Moveables. 120

Using Draggable Handles 122

Responding to Drag Events 124

Using Multiple Moveables. 126

 Setting Motion Limits 128

Using Source to Drag HTML Elements 130

Handling Events with Source. 132

TABLE OF CONTENTS

Chapter 8: Animation and Special Effects   135

Using Fades. 136

Controlling Fade Speed with Functions. 138

Sliding Elements. 140

Wiping Elements 142

Expanding Elements. 144

Controlling Expansion Speed with Functions. . . 146

Animating Drag-and-Drop Operations 148

Toggling Elements Between Visible
and Invisible 150

Blending Colors. 152

Chapter 9: Ajax   155

Using Ajax Without Dojo. 156

Using the Dojo xhrGet Method. 158

Using Dojo xhrGet to Read XML. 160

Using Dojo xhrGet to Read JSON 162

Handling Dojo xhrGet Errors. 164

Sending Data Using GET. 166

Using GET with Forms 168

Sending Data Using POST. 170

Chapter 10: Advanced Ajax   173

Handling Ajax Timeouts 174

Getting Error Messages 176

Finishing Ajax Operations. 178

Preventing Caching. 180

Making Ajax Operations Synchronous. 182

Getting the XMLHttpRequest Object 184

Getting Header Data. 186

Creating Callback Chains 188

Canceling a Chained Request 190

Index   193

INTRODUCTION

Welcome to the Dojo Toolkit: an open-source JavaScript toolkit for building Web applications so dynamic they jump off the page. Filled with special controls such as calendars and menus, and special effects such as wipes and fade-ins, Dojo is gaining popularity rapidly.

Perhaps most important, Dojo is emerging as the toolkit of choice for Ajax applications. Ajax is a set of techniques that allows you to access a Web server from a browser without a page refresh—that is, there's no blinking and no flicker when you download data behind the scenes with Ajax; you just download the data, and then you can display it in a Web page using dynamic HTML processes. No fuss, no muss—and the end result is an application that looks more like a desktop application than a Web application. With Ajax, the user can do something in a browser page, and the result of the operation appears instantly in the browser window, immediately updating the page without affecting the other contents of the window.

Ajax has often been referred to as the future of Web applications, and Dojo is becoming the way to go when implementing Ajax.

What's in This Book

Dojo is a JavaScript toolkit, which means that it's prewritten JavaScript, ready for you to put to work in your own Web pages. In this book, you'll get a guided tour of the tools that make Dojo so popular.

We start with a look at the controls that come with Dojo, such as clickable calendars and accordion containers that expand and contract at the click of a button. These controls, called Dijits in Dojo, are among Dojo's most popular features. The Dijits have a polished, professional look and are available for just about any purpose you can think of in Web pages. This book provides a survey of the Dojo Dijits, putting them to work and showing you how they do what they do.

Dojo is known for its drag-and-drop capability, which enables you to drag elements in a Web page to new locations with the mouse and then drop them there. Although you can write this functionality in JavaScript yourself, getting it to work across different browsers and different browser versions is hard—except when you use Dojo.

Dojo is also known for its visual effects, including slick-looking wipes, in which a sheet of color wipes over an element, and fades, in which an element and its background fade from view. You'll see how to use these kinds of effects in your Web pages.

This book concludes with two chapters on Ajax: one that provides you with basic skills, and one that gets you into truly advanced territory. When you finish this book, you'll be an expert on using Ajax with Dojo.

That's the game plan then: to put Dojo to work and see it at its most impressive.

What You'll Need

You don't need much to use this book besides a knowledge of HTML, some knowledge of JavaScript, and a Web browser.

In Chapter 1, you'll see how to install Dojo—and that you don't even need to install it to use it.

Nearly all the examples in this book can be run from your hard disk simply by opening them in a browser. You should be fairly familiar with basic JavaScript, however. If you're not, take a look at a good online tutorial before proceeding.

A few Ajax examples make use of PHP on the server, and those examples need to be placed on a Web server that supports the PHP online scripting language. However, you don't need to know PHP to read this book: those examples only demonstrate how to verify that you can send data to the Web server as well as download it using Ajax; if you don't have access to a PHP-enabled Web server, you can simply skip those examples.

You can download the examples in this book from www.peachpit.com/dojovqs. To access this supplementary content, you'll need to register this product. Go to www.peachpit.com/dojovqs. Log in or join Peachpit.com and enter the book's ISBN (0321605128). After you register, a link to the supplemental content will be listed on your Account page.

ESSENTIAL DOJO

Dojo is the premier JavaScript toolkit for use in Web pages. It gives you just about all the power you can squeeze out of JavaScript, providing powerful new controls (colorpickers, text box validation, menus, dialog boxes, calendars, and more).

Dojo also smoothes out the differences between browsers, eliminating all the annoying differences between browsers that JavaScript programmers have to deal with otherwise. You can use it in many different types of browsers without changing your code—that's a major attraction of Dojo.

We'll start with an overview of Dojo to get oriented. As this book progresses, we'll look at the controls Dijit offers and then move up to Ajax, animation, and more.

About Dojo

Dojo consists of several parts.

Dojo's Core and Base packages together handle such popular features as animation, dragging and dropping, cookies, and Asynchronous JavaScript and XML (Ajax). Ajax allows you to interact with the Web server without causing a screen refresh in the browser, which gives Web applications a desktop application feel. Dojo is emerging as the standard tool for working with Ajax.

Dijit is Dojo's extremely popular library of widgets, offering Web page controls for the user to interact with. The Dojo widgets can be styled, and they augment what comes standard in a browser.

We'll see all these and more in this book. After Ajax, Dijits are the most popular reason for using Dojo.

The Dojo Extensions, or Dojox, package is where you'll find the cutting-edge features (and more are being added all the time), such as controls that let you graph your data in grids and charts (which are integrated with the Dojo Data package for true database power). Dojox also includes tools to take your Web page offline and still keep it working, as well as to perform 2D and 3D drawing.

Dojo's Util package provides dozens of utility functions that augment JavaScript, such as functions that work on strings and XML.

That's what Dojo looks like from 20,000 feet. Now we'll start digging into it to see what it actually offers us.

Figure 1.1 The official Dojo Web site.

Getting Dojo

You don't need to download Dojo to run the examples in this book (our Web pages will pick up Dojo online)—or even to use Dojo (you can use the same trick as we do in this book). However, most users do download and install Dojo. You can then upload it to your Internet service provider (ISP).

You can download Dojo for free at http://www.dojotoolkit.com/ (**Figure 1.1**).

To get and install Dojo:

1. In your browser, navigate to http://download.dojotoolkit.org/current-stable/ (**Figure 1.2**).

2. Right-click the compressed Dojo release file right for your system: dojo-release-1.1.1.zip if you can use .zip files or dojo-release-1.1.1.tar.gz if you can handle .tar.gz files (use the most current version). Then click Save Target As (Internet Explorer) or Save Link As (Firefox) in the menu that appears.

3. In the dialog box that opens, click Save to save the compressed file to your hard disk.

4. Uncompress the compressed file.

   This creates a new folder named dojo-release-*x.y.z* (*x.y.z* will be the version number, such as 1.1.1) that contains four subfolders: dojo (for Base and Core), dijit, dojox, and util.

✔ Tip

■ The folder name dojo-release-*x.y.z* is pretty awkward, and it will appear in all your Web pages. You can rename that folder, using something shorter, such as javascript, but you don't have to.

Figure 1.2 The official Dojo downloads page; you get Dojo here.

Index of /current-stable

Name	Last modified	Size
Parent Directory		-
dojo-release-1.1.1-mini.tar.gz	12-May-2008 18:36	1.1M
dojo-release-1.1.1-mini.tar.gz.md5	12-May-2008 18:36	72
dojo-release-1.1.1-shrinksafe.tar.gz	12-May-2008 12:26	780K
dojo-release-1.1.1-shrinksafe.tar.gz.md5	12-May-2008 12:26	71
dojo-release-1.1.1-shrinksafe.zip	12-May-2008 12:26	781K
dojo-release-1.1.1-shrinksafe.zip.md5	12-May-2008 12:26	68
dojo-release-1.1.1-src.tar.gz	12-May-2008 12:26	15M
dojo-release-1.1.1-src.tar.gz.md5	12-May-2008 12:26	64
dojo-release-1.1.1-src.zip	12-May-2008 12:26	16M
dojo-release-1.1.1-src.zip.md5	12-May-2008 12:26	61
dojo-release-1.1.1.tar.gz	12-May-2008 12:26	4.1M
dojo-release-1.1.1.tar.gz.md5	12-May-2008 12:26	60
dojo-release-1.1.1.zip	12-May-2008 12:26	5.1M
dojo-release-1.1.1.zip.md5	12-May-2008 12:26	57
dojo-release-1.1.1/	12-May-2008 15:36	-

5. Upload the dojo-release-*x.y.z* folder and all its contents to your ISP, to the folder where your Web pages will be stored.

If, for example, you store your Web pages in a folder named home, this step creates a new folder, home/dojo-release-*x.y.z*. If you don't store your Web pages in a folder but instead in the root directory, this step creates a new folder named dojo-release-*x.y.z* in your root directory.

Dojo is now installed and accessible to your Web pages.

You can load the main Dojo JavaScript file (where Dojo is concentrated), dojo.js, using a `<script>` element like this (substitute the current version number, such as 1.1.1, for *x.y.z*):

```
<script

  type="text/javascript"

  src="dojo-release-x.y.z/dojo/dojo.
   → js">

</script>
```

If you've renamed the dojo-release-*x.y.z* folder javascript, the code should look like this:

```
<script

  type="text/javascript"

  src="javascript/dojo/dojo.js">

</script>
```

We'll put this code to work in a few pages.

✔ Tip

■ If you're unsure about how to upload files to your ISP, contact your ISP's tech team. You use the same method—FTP or HTML— that you use to upload your Web pages.

Using AOL CDN to Get Dojo

If you've installed Dojo as described in the previous section, you can load it into your Web pages (so you can access Dojo using JavaScript).

However, you can also access Dojo without having to download it at all: you can get it from the AOL Content Delivery Network (CDN).

Getting dojo.js from the AOL content network has one big advantage: you don't have to install Dojo on your ISP to use it. This book does not assume that you've installed Dojo—most examples use the AOL CDN so they run immediately, no Dojo installation necessary.

To get Dojo from the AOL CDN:

◆ If you don't want to download Dojo yourself, you can get Dojo into your page using this URL in a `<script>` element:

```
<script
  type="text/javascript"
  src="http://o.aolcdn.com/
    dojo/1.1/dojo/dojo.xd.js">
</script>
```

✔ Tips

■ The main Dojo JavaScript file, dojo.js, is called dojo.xd.js (xd stands for cross-domain) in the AOL CDN.

■ The URL for dojo.xd.js, http://o.aolcdn.com/dojo/1.1/dojo/dojo.xd.js, is broken onto two lines in this book, but make sure it's on one line in your code.

■ The URL for dojo.xd.js references Dojo version 1.1, but the current version is actually 1.1.1. That's OK—referencing the current version's major and minor numbers (1.1) gives you the latest update version (1.1.1 in this case).

Getting Started with Dojo

We'll start our tour of Dojo with Dijit. You'll add the Dojo JavaScript libraries to a Web page and place two Dijits on that page. After you have the page Dojo enabled and a few Dijits working, you can use that page as a template for other Dojo-enabled pages.

Our goal in this chapter is shown in **Figure 1.3**. That's a Dojo-enabled page, textbox. html, with two Dijits: a button and a text box (although the HTML text control is called a text field, in Dojo it is a text box).

To prove that the Web page is functional, when you click the button, the message "Welcome to Dojo" appears in the text box (**Figure 1.4**).

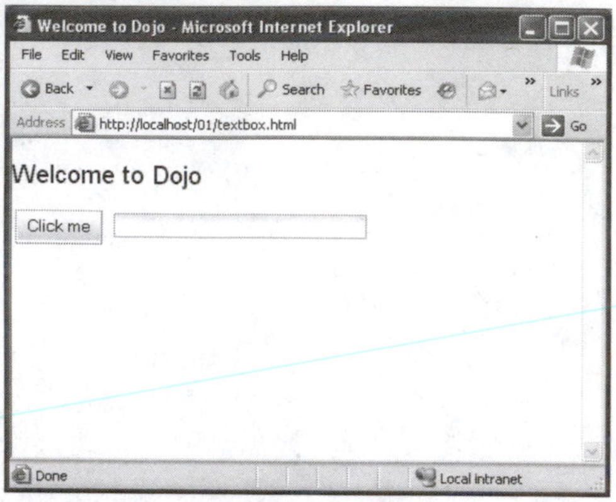

✔ Tip

■ You can download all the code from this book from the book's Web site. That code is divided into folders according to the chapter number, so you'll find textbox. html listed as 01/textbox.html in the downloadable code.

Figure 1.3 The Dojo-enabled page that we're going to create in this chapter.

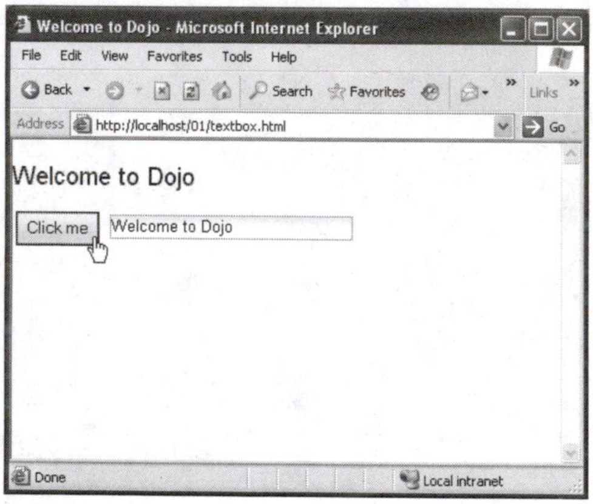

Figure 1.4 When you click the button, a message appears in the text box, showing that the page is functional.

Script 1.1 Beginning a Dojo page.

```
1    <html>
2      <head>
3        <title>Welcome to Dojo</title>
4        <script
5          type="text/javascript"
6          src="http://o.aolcdn.com/dojo/1.1/
7            dojo/dojo.xd.js">
8        </script>
9      <head>
10     <body>
11       <h1>Welcome to Dojo</h1>
12       <br>
13       <button
14         id="button"
15         Click me
16       </button>
17       <input
18         id="text"
19         type="text"
20       </input>
21       <br>
22     </body>
23   </html>
```

Script 1.2 Beginning a Dojo page with Dojo installed on your system.

```
1    <script
2      djConfig="parseOnLoad:true"
3      type="text/javascript"
4      src="dojo-release-x.y.z/dojo/dojo.js">
5    </script>
```

Creating a Dojo Web Page

We'll start putting together the page shown in Figure 1.4: the simple Dojo page that has a button and a text box.

To begin a Dojo page:

1. Open a text editor (such as Microsoft WordPad) to create your Web page. We'll use the example textbox.html here.

2. Enter your code.
   - ▲ Enter the code for textbox.html, shown in **Script 1.1**. The highlighted code is what's essential to load Dojo in the page.
   - ▲ If you've installed Dojo yourself, enter the <script> element as shown in **Script 1.2** (replace $x.y.z$ with the current version).

3. Save the file.

✔ Tip

■ When you save the file, make sure you select Text Document in the Save as Type dialog box. Don't inadvertently save the file in RTF format, which is the default format of Windows WordPad.

Using the Dojo Styles

Dojo specializes in snappy-looking Web pages, and they get to be snappy by using the Dojo style sheets, such as dojo.css. Three style themes come with Dojo:

◆ Tundra: Mostly light gray and light blue.

◆ Soria: Mostly light blue on blue; Dijits have a glossy look.

◆ Nihilo: Mostly white with light gray outlines.

✔ Tip

■ A theme specifies styles for all parts of a page and the Dijits on it.

To use a Dojo theme:

1. Open your Web page, such as textbox. html, in a text editor.

2. To use a Dojo theme such as Tundra, include dojo.css on your page as well as the theme-specific CSS file: tundra.css in this case. Then assign the style attribute in the page's <body> element to the theme's name ("tundra" in this case).

   ▲ Enter the highlighted code shown in **Script 1.3** for textbox.html.

Script 1.3 Using a Dojo theme.

```
1   <html>
2     <head>
3       <title>Welcome to Dojo</title>
4
5       <link rel="stylesheet"
6         type="text/css"
7         href="http://o.aolcdn.com/
8         dojo/1.1/dojo/
9         resources/dojo.css" />
10
11      <link rel="stylesheet"
12        type="text/css"
13        href="http://o.aolcdn.com/dojo/
14        1.1/dijit/
15        themes/tundra/tundra.css" />
16
17      <script
18        djConfig="parseOnLoad:true"
19        type="text/javascript"
20        src="http://o.aolcdn.com/dojo/1.1/
21          dojo/dojo.xd.js">
22      </script>
23    <head>
24
25    <body class="tundra">
26      <h1>Welcome to Dojo</h1>
27      <br>
28      <button
29        id="button"
30        Click me
31      </button>
32
33      <input
34        id="text"
35        type="text"
36        maxlength="25"
37      </input>
38      <br>
39    </body>
40  </html>
```

Script 1.4 Using a Dojo theme with Dojo installed on your system.

```
         ⊖ ⊖ ⊖                     script
1    <link rel="stylesheet"
2      type="text/css"
3      href="dojo-release-
4       x.y.z/dojo/resources/dojo.css" />
5    <link rel="stylesheet"
6      type="text/css"
7      href="dojo-release-
8       x.y.z/dijit/themes/tundra/tundra.css" />
```

▲ If you've installed Dojo yourself, enter the <link> elements as shown in **Script 1.4** (replace *x.y.z* with the current version).

3. Save your file.

Now the Dijits you create in the page will use the Tundra theme.

✔ Tip

■ Tundra is probably the most commonly used Dojo theme. But give the others a try as well, to see which you like best.

Preparing to Use Dijits

To use Dojo Dijits, you have to make sure that Dojo *parses* (that is, reads) your Web page so it knows about those Dijits. If you don't parse the Web page, the Dijits will act as only normal HTML controls at best, because Dojo won't know about them. So in every Dojo-enabled page that uses Dijits, you must load the Dojo parser and indicate that you want to parse the page.

To connect Dijits to Dojo:

1. Open your Web page, such as textbox. html, in a text editor.

2. To include the Dojo parser in the Web page, add the JavaScript `dojo.require("dojo.parser")`. to a `<script>` element in your page.

3. In the opening tag of the `<script>` element where you load dojo.js or dojo.xd.js, include the attribute `djconfig` and set it to `true` to make Dojo parse the page.

   Script 1.5 shows what your page should look like after you enter the highlighted code.

4. Save your file.

✔ Tips

- The `djconfig` attribute means "Dojo configuration," and this is our first use of it. We'll use it throughout the book to configure Dojo in other ways as well.

- The `dojo.require` statement is what you use to include the various Dojo modules in your code. Requiring a module adds it to your page and makes it accessible in JavaScript.

Script 1.5 Connecting Dijits to Dojo.

```
1   <html>
2     <head>
3       <title>Welcome to Dojo</title>
4
5       <link rel="stylesheet"
6         type="text/css"
7         href="http://o.aolcdn.com/
8         dojo/1.1/dojo/
9         resources/dojo.css" />
10
11      <link rel="stylesheet"
12        type="text/css"
13        href="http://o.aolcdn.com/dojo/
14        1.1/dijit/
15        themes/tundra/tundra.css" />
16
17      <script
18        djConfig="parseOnLoad:true"
19        type="text/javascript"
20        src="http://o.aolcdn.com/dojo/1.1/
21          dojo/dojo.xd.js">
22      </script>
23
24      <script type="text/javascript">
25        dojo.require("dojo.parser");
26      </script>
27    <head>
28
29    <body class="tundra">
30      <h1>Welcome to Dojo</h1>
31      <br>
32      <button
33        id="button"
34        Click me
35      </button>
36
37      <input
38        id="text"
39        type="text"
40        name="text"
41        maxlength="25"
42      </input>
43      <br>
44    </body>
45  </html>
```

Script 1.6 Creating a Dojo button.

```
 1    <html>
 2     <head>
 3       <title>Welcome to Dojo</title>
 4
 5       <link rel="stylesheet"
 6         type="text/css"
 7         href="http://o.aolcdn.com/
 8         dojo/1.1/dojo/
 9         resources/dojo.css" />
10
11       <link rel="stylesheet"
12         type="text/css"
13         href="http://o.aolcdn.com/dojo/
14         1.1/dijit/
15         themes/tundra/tundra.css" />
16
17       <script
18         djConfig="parseOnLoad:true"
19         type="text/javascript"
20         src="http://o.aolcdn.com/dojo/1.1/
21           dojo/dojo.xd.js">
22       </script>
23
24       <script type="text/javascript">
25         dojo.require("dojo.parser");
26         dojo.require("dijit.form.Button");
27
28       </script>
29     <head>
30
31     <body class="tundra">
32       <h1>Welcome to Dojo</h1>
33       <br>
34     <button
35         id="button"
36         dojoType="dijit.form.Button">
37         Click me
38       </button>
39
40       <input
41         id="text"
42         type="text"
43         name="text"
44         maxlength="25"
45       </input>
46       <br>
47     </body>
48    </html>
```

Adding a Button Dijit

Dijits are based on HTML elements, and you tell Dojo that you want a particular HTML element to be a Dijit by using the `dojoType` attribute. In this task, you'll see how to convert an HTML button to a Dijit button.

To create a Dojo button:

1. Open your Web page, such as textbox. html, in a text editor.

2. Modify any buttons in your Web page so their opening tag contains the attribute `dojoType="dijit.form.Button"`.

3. Use the `dojo.require` statement to include the Dojo module `"dijit.form. Button"`, which contains the JavaScript support for button Dijits.

   Script 1.6 shows what your page should look like after you enter the highlighted code.

4. Save your file.

Now when Dojo parses the page, it will replace that HTML button with the Dijit version automatically.

✔ Tip

■ Don't forget the `form` in `"dijit.form. Button"`. Many novices try to require `"dijit.Button"` and then are surprised when the code doesn't work. In fact, the Button module is a submodule of the `dijit.form` module—which is why buttons are considered form controls in Dijit.

Adding a TextBox Dijit

You can add a Dijit text box converting an existing HTML text box into a TextBox Dijit. Here, we'll convert the text box in textbox.html into a TextBox Dijit.

To create a Dojo text box:

1. Open your Web page, such as textbox.html, in a text editor.

2. Modify any text boxes in your Web page so their opening tag contains the attribute dojoType="dijit.form.TextBox".

3. Use the dojo.require statement to include the Dojo module "dijit.form.TextBox", which contains the JavaScript support for Dijit text boxes.

   Script 1.7 shows how your page should look after you enter the highlighted code.

4. Save your file.

You've converted the HTML text box in the page to a TextBox Dijit.

✔ Tip

■ This example uses just a simple text box, but as you'll see in the next chapter, Dojo contains many variations on simple text boxes: ValidationTextBox, RangeBoundTextBox, DateTimeTextBox, NumberTextBox, CurrencyTextBox, NumberSpinner, and more.

Script 1.7 Creating a Dojo text box.

```
1    <html>
2      <head>
3        <title>Welcome to Dojo</title>
4
5        <link rel="stylesheet"
6          type="text/css"
7          href="http://o.aolcdn.com/
8          dojo/1.1/dojo/
9          resources/dojo.css" />
10
11       <link rel="stylesheet"
12         type="text/css"
13         href="http://o.aolcdn.com/dojo/
14         1.1/dijit/
15         themes/tundra/tundra.css" />
16
17       <script
18         djConfig="parseOnLoad:true"
19         type="text/javascript"
20         src="http://o.aolcdn.com/dojo/1.1/
21           dojo/dojo.xd.js">
22       </script>
23
24       <script type="text/javascript">
25         dojo.require("dojo.parser");
26         dojo.require("dijit.form.Button");
27         dojo.require("dijit.form.TextBox");
28
29       </script>
30     <head>
31
32     <body class="tundra">
33       <h1>Welcome to Dojo</h1>
34       <br>
35       <button
36         id="button"
37         dojoType="dijit.form.Button">
38         Click me
39       </button>
40
41       <input id="text" type="text"
42         name="text"
43         maxlength="25"
44         dojoType="dijit.form.TextBox">
45       </input>
46       <br>
47     </body>
48   </html>
```

Script 1.8 Handling Dijit events.

```
1   <html>
2     <head>
3       <title>Welcome to Dojo</title>
4
5       <link rel="stylesheet"
6         type="text/css"
7         href="http://o.aolcdn.com/
8         dojo/1.1/dojo/
9         resources/dojo.css" />
10
11      <link rel="stylesheet"
12        type="text/css"
13        href="http://o.aolcdn.com/dojo/
14        1.1/dijit/
15        themes/tundra/tundra.css" />
16
17      <script
18        djConfig="parseOnLoad:true"
19        type="text/javascript"
20        src="http://o.aolcdn.com/dojo/1.1/
21          dojo/dojo.xd.js">
22      </script>
23
24      <script type="text/javascript">
25        dojo.require("dojo.parser");
26        dojo.require("dijit.form.Button");
27        dojo.require("dijit.form.TextBox");
28
29        dojo.addOnLoad(function(){
30          dojo.connect(
31          Dijit.
32          Event
33          Function
34          );
35        });
36      </script>
37    <head>
38
39    <body class="tundra">
40      <h1>Welcome to Dojo</h1>
41      <br>
42      <button
43        id="button"
44        dojoType="dijit.form.Button">
45        Click me
46      </button>
47
48      <input id="text" type="text"
49        name="text"
50        maxlength="25"
51        dojoType="dijit.form.TextBox">
52      </input>
53      <br>
54    </body>
55  </html>
```

Responding to Dijit Events

You can respond to Dijit events, such as a button click, by connecting the event to a JavaScript function.

The trick is that you need to wait until the page is fully loaded before you start accessing Dijits in code. If you try to work with a Dijit in code before it's fully loaded, the browser will not see the Dijit you want to work with and cause an error. To wait until the page is fully loaded before working with the Dijits in the page, you use the Dojo method dojo.addOnLoad; you pass that method a JavaScript function to call when the page is fully loaded.

To actually connect a Dijit to JavaScript code to respond to events such as button clicks, you use the dojo.connect method.

To handle Dijit events:

1. Open your Web page, such as textbox. html, in a text editor.

2. Pass an anonymous JavaScript function to dojo.addOnLoad, causing that function to be executed when the page is fully loaded.

3. Use the dojo.connect method to start the process of connecting a Dijit to JavaScript code that should execute when one of the Dijit's events occurs.

   To the dojo.connect method, you pass the Dijit whose event you want to connect, the event to be connected, and the function that should be called when the event occurs.

   Script 1.8 shows what your page should look like after you enter the highlighted code (note that the items in italics are placeholders; you'll see how to replace them with actual code in the next section).

4. Save your file.

In the next section, we'll see an example of the dojo.connect method in action.

13

Displaying Text In a Text Box After a Button Click

To display text in a Dijit text box when a button is clicked, you can connect the button to the text box with the `dojo.connect` method. You get Dijit objects corresponding to the button and text box using the `dojo.byId` method. You pass this method the ID of a Dijit, and it returns an object corresponding to the Dijit. You set the text in a text box with the `setValue` method.

To place text in a text box when the user clicks a button:

1. Open your Web page, such as textbox. html, in a text editor.

   You need to pass the `dojo.connect` method an object corresponding to the button, the event you want to handle, and the function you want to execute when that event occurs.

2. The ID of the button is "`button`", so use the expression `dojo.byId("button")` to pass the `dojo.connect` method an object corresponding to the button.

3. Pass the `dojo.connect` method the string "`onClick`" to indicate that you want to handle the `onClick` event.

Script 1.9 Placing text in a text box when the user clicks a button.

```
1    <html>
2      <head>
3        <title>Welcome to Dojo</title>
4
5        <link rel="stylesheet"
6          type="text/css"
7          href="http://o.aolcdn.com/
8          dojo/1.1/dojo/
9          resources/dojo.css" />
10
11       <link rel="stylesheet"
12         type="text/css"
13         href="http://o.aolcdn.com/dojo/
14         1.1/dijit/
15         themes/tundra/tundra.css" />
16
17       <script
18         djConfig="parseOnLoad:true"
19         type="text/javascript"
20         src="http://o.aolcdn.com/dojo/1.1/
21           dojo/dojo.xd.js">
22       </script>
23
24       <script type="text/javascript">
25         dojo.require("dojo.parser");
26         dojo.require("dijit.form.Button");
27         dojo.require("dijit.form.TextBox");
28
29         dojo.addOnLoad(function(){
30           dojo.connect(
31             dijit.byId("button"),
32             "onClick", function(evt) {
33             dijit.byId(
34               "text").setValue(
35               "Welcome to Dojo");
36           });
37         });
38       </script>
39     <head>
40
41     <body class="tundra">
```

(script continues)

4. Pass the `dojo.connect` method an anonymous JavaScript function that uses the text box's `setValue` method to set the text box's text to "Welcome to Dojo." The anonymous function will be passed a Dijit Event object (covered in detail in the next chapter), which we won't use here.

Script 1.9 shows how your page should look after you enter the highlighted code.

5. Save your file.

✔ Tip

■ Unlike HTML, Dijit is sensitive to capitalization of Dijit event names, so, for instance, be sure to enter "onClick", not "onclick".

Script 1.9 *continued*

```
42         <h1>Welcome to Dojo</h1>
43         <br>
44         <button
45           id="button"
46           dojoType="dijit.form.Button">
47           Click me
48         </button>
49
50         <input id="text" type="text"
51           name="text"
52           maxlength="25"
53           dojoType="dijit.form.TextBox">
54         </input>
55         <br>
56       </body>
57     </html>
```

Running textbox.html

You've completed textbox.html. Running it is easy—just open it in a browser.

To run textbox.html in a browser:

1. Save textbox.html on your hard disk or ISP.

2. Open your browser and navigate to textbox.html.

   ▲ If textbox.html is on your hard disk, choose File > Open (in Internet Explorer) or File > Open File (in Firefox).

   ▲ If the file is on your ISP, enter the appropriate URL in your browser's address box.

   If you're opening textbox.html from your hard disk and are using Internet Explorer, a warning security bar may appear at the top of the browser window with a message similar to this: "To help protect your security, Internet Explorer has restricted this file from showing active content that could access your computer. Click here for options." Click the bar and from the menu select Allow Blocked Content; then click Yes in the dialog box that opens to enable JavaScript in this example.

3. Click the Click Me button.

   You should see the "Welcome to Dojo" message appear in the text box, as shown in Figure 1.4.

Congratulations—you've created a fully functional Dojo page.

✔ Tip

■ If you can't get this example to work correctly, verify that the `<script>` and `<link>` elements are accessing Dojo (for example, if you've installed Dojo, make sure that it was installed at the location where you're telling your browser to look for it). Another common error is to save textbox.html in RTF format inadvertently, because that's the default format of Windows WordPad. When you save the file, make sure you select Text Document in the Save as Type dialog box.

Form Dijits: Text Boxes and Buttons

In the previous chapter, we got Dojo and Dijit up and running. In this chapter, we'll work with two fundamental Dijits: buttons and text boxes. Working with these two basic Dijits will help you build your foundation of Dijit skills.

Both buttons and text boxes have many variations in Dojo: for example, in addition to the standard TextBox Dijit that you saw in Chapter 1, you can insert ValidationTextBox Dijits, which let you build in validation that checks what a user enters, as the user enters it. You can also insert date and time controls that descend from text boxes, number spinners that let users click up and down arrows to select numbers, and more.

In Chapter 1, we created our Dijits with HTML `<input>` elements. However, you can also create Dijits entirely using JavaScript. You can also connect JavaScript functions to Dijits using `<script>` elements instead of the `connect` method, add debugging displays to your pages, submit pages to Web servers, and more.

All of these topics are coming up in this chapter.

Creating Dijits in Code

In Chapter 1, we created our Dijits with HTML elements, like this, which creates a TextBox Dijit:

```
<input id="text" type="text"
  maxlength="25"
  dojoType="dijit.form.TextBox">
</input>
```

But in Dojo, you can also create Dijits using JavaScript. To do that, you use the fully qualified name of the Dijit (such as dijit.form. TextBox) as a constructor, passing it an associative array of parameters (that is, a comma-separated list of *name* : *value* pairs, enclosed in curly braces) and the ID (as a text string) of the existing HTML element you want to replace. We'll look at an example, textbox-program.html, now.

To create Dijits in code:

1. Open your Web page, such as textbox-program.html, in a text editor.

2. Create a TextBox Dijit to replace the HTML <input> element with the ID "text", passing the new TextBox parameters that give it the length of 25 characters and the ID "text2" by entering the code shown in **Script 2.1**.

Script 2.1 Creating Dijits in code.

```
1    <html>
2      <head>
3        <title>Creating Dijits in Code</title>
4
5        <link rel="stylesheet"
6          type="text/css"
7          href="http://o.aolcdn.com/
8          dojo/1.1/dojo/
9          resources/dojo.css" />
10
11       <link rel="stylesheet"
12         type="text/css"
13         href="http://o.aolcdn.com/dojo/
14         1.1/dijit/
15         themes/tundra/tundra.css" />
16
17       <script
18         djConfig="parseOnLoad:true"
19         type="text/javascript"
20         src="http://o.aolcdn.com/dojo/1.1/
21         dojo/dojo.xd.js">
22       </script>
23
24       <script type="text/javascript">
25         dojo.require("dojo.parser");
26         dojo.require("dijit.form.Button");
27         dojo.require("dijit.form.TextBox");
28
29         dojo.addOnLoad(function( ) {
30           var t = new dijit.form.TextBox({
31             length : 25,
32             id : "text2"},
33             "text");
34
35           dojo.connect(dijit.byId("button"),
36             "onClick", function(evt) {
37             dijit.byId("text2").setValue(
38             "Welcome to Dojo");
39           });
40         });
41       </script>
42     <head>
43
44     <body class="tundra">
45       <h1>Creating Dijits in Code</h1>
46       <br>
47       <button id="button"
48         dojoType="dijit.form.Button">Click me
49       </button>
50       <input id="text"></input>
51     </body>
52   </html>
```

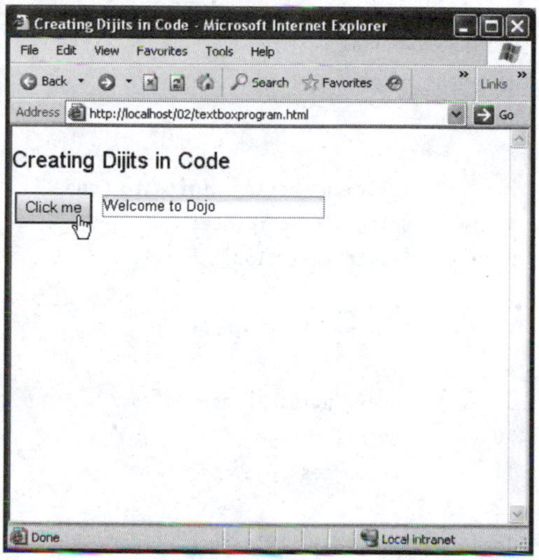

Figure 2.1 Displaying a message in a text box created with JavaScript code.

3. Save your file.

4. Navigate to your file in a browser. You should see a button and a text box.

5. Click the button. The message should appear in the text box (**Figure 2.1**).

✔ Tip

■ Don't refer to the Dijit you create in code (for example, in a call to the connect method) until after you've created it, or the browser won't be able to find it.

Connecting Code to Dijits Using <script> Elements

In Chapter 1, we connected buttons to the JavaScript code that used the connect method. Here's what that looked like when we connected a button's onClick event to an anonymous function that displayed a message in a text box:

```
dojo.connect(dijit.byId("button"),
  "onClick", function(evt) {
  dijit.byId("text2").setValue(
  "Welcome to Dojo");
});
```

However, with Dojo you can also connect JavaScript code to Dijits using <script> elements—no connect method needed. We'll look at how that works in an example named textboxscript.html.

To connect JavaScript to Dijits using <script> elements:

1. Open your Web page, such as textbox-script.html, in a text editor.

2. Embed a <script> element inside a <button> element, setting the type attribute to "dojo/method", the event attribute to "onClick", and the args attribute to "evt" (this is the argument that will be passed to the enclosed JavaScript—a Dojo Event object in this case).

3. Enclose the JavaScript you want run when the button is clicked inside the <script> element. In this case, that JavaScript will display a message in a text box.

   Script 2.2 shows what your page should look like after you make the additions.

Script 2.2 Connecting JavaScript to Dijits using <script> elements.

```
1    <html>
2     <head>
3      <title>Connecting Dijits to Code
4       Using &lt;script&gt;
5       Elements</title>
6
7      <link rel="stylesheet"
8       type="text/css"
9       href="http://o.aolcdn.com/
10      dojo/1.1/dojo/
11      resources/dojo.css" />
12
13      <link rel="stylesheet"
14       type="text/css"
15       href="http://o.aolcdn.com/dojo/
16      1.1/dijit/
17      themes/tundra/tundra.css" />
18
19      <script
20       djConfig="parseOnLoad:true"
21       type="text/javascript"
22       src="http://o.aolcdn.com/dojo/1.1/
23        dojo/dojo.xd.js">
24      </script>
25
26      <script type="text/javascript">
27       dojo.require("dojo.parser");
28       dojo.require("dijit.form.Button");
29       dojo.require("dijit.form.TextBox");
30
31       dojo.addOnLoad(function( ) {
32        var t = new dijit.form.TextBox({
33         length : 25,
34         id : "text"
35        }, "text");
36       });
37      </script>
38     <head>
39
40     <body class="tundra">
41      <h1>Connecting Dijits to Code Using
```

(script continues)

Script 2.2 *continued*

```
42          &lt;script&gt; Elements</h1>
43      <br>
44      <button id="button"
45      dojoType="dijit.form.Button">
46        Click me
47        <script type="dojo/method"
48        event="onClick" args="evt">
49         dijit.byId("text").setValue(
50          "Welcome to Dojo");
51        </script>
52      </button>
53      <input id="text"></input>
54    </body>
55  </html>
```

4. Save your file.

5. Navigate to your file in a browser. You should see a button and a text box.

6. Click the button, which should make the message appear in the text box (**Figure 2.2**).

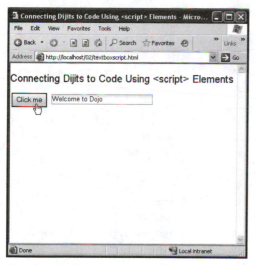

Figure 2.2 Displaying a message in a text box connected to a button with a <script> element.

Submitting to Web Sites

So far, the Dijit examples you've seen have all been contained in the same page. You click a button, and a message appears in a text box. However, Web pages with controls such as buttons and text boxes often communicate with programs online.

Using the example textboxsubmit.html, you'll submit the data that a user has entered in controls in a Dojo-enabled page. You'll send the data to a script reflect.php, written in the PHP scripting language, which will echo the data it receives (you don't have to know PHP to use this example).

To send data to a Web site from a Dojo-enabled page:

1. Open your Web page, such as textboxsubmit.html, in a text editor.

2. Add a new <form> element with the method attribute set to "POST", the dojoType attribute set to "dijit.form.Form" (it's not necessary to make the form a Dijit form, but doing so allows you to use Dijit methods on the form if you want to), and the action attribute "http://localhost/02/reflect.php" so the form will send data to reflect.php (substitute the actual URL for reflect.php here).

3. Add a dojo.require statement to require dojo.form.Form.

4. Give a button in the form the dojoType attribute "dijit.form.Button" and the type attribute "submit".

   Script 2.3 shows what your page should look like after you make the additions.

Script 2.3 Sending data to a Web site from a Dojo-enabled page.

```
1    <html>
2      <head>
3        <title>Submitting data online</title>
(4–18)  . . .
19       <script type="text/javascript">
20         dojo.require("dojo.parser");
21         dojo.require("dijit.form.TextBox");
22         dojo.require("dijit.form.Button");
23         dojo.require("dijit.form.Form");
24       </script>
25     </head>
26
27     <body class="tundra">
28       <h1>Submitting data online</h1>
29             <br>
30       <form
31         dojoType="dijit.form.Form"
32         method="POST"
33         action =
34         "http://localhost/02/reflect.php">
35         Enter your name:
36         <input
37           dojoType="dijit.form.TextBox"
38           name="text"
39           id="text">
40         </input>
41
42         <button
43           type="submit"
44           dojoType="dijit.form.Button">
45           Submit
46         </button>
47       </form>
48     </body>
49   </html>
```

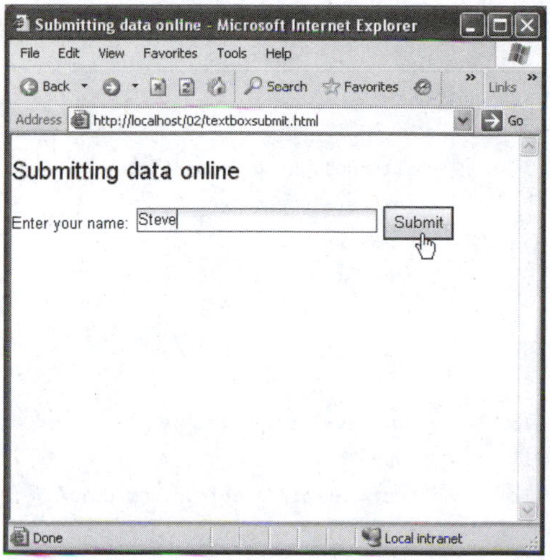

Figure 2.3 Entering a name.

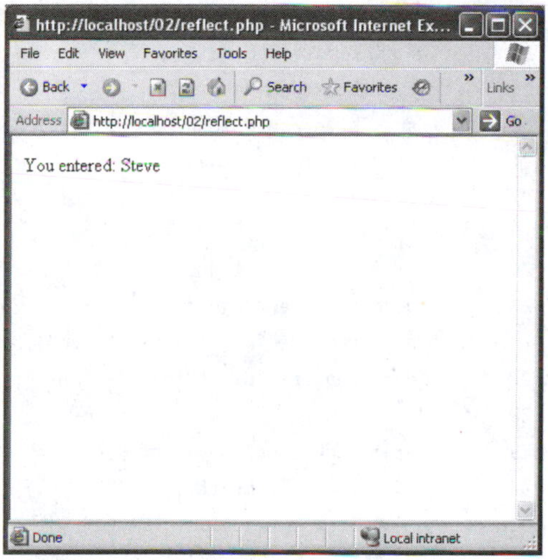

Figure 2.4 The submitted name displayed.

5. Save your file.

6. Create a new file, reflect.php, at a URL that your browser can access (the same location pointed to by the `action` attribute of the form) in an environment (such as an ISP) that can run PHP.

7. Give reflect.php these contents:

```php
<?php
echo "You entered: " . $_
REQUEST["text"];
?>
```

8. Save reflect.php.

9. Navigate to the HTML file in a browser. You should see a button and a text box.

10. Enter your name in the text box (**Figure 2.3**).

11. Click the button. Your name should appear, displayed by reflect.php (**Figure 2.4**).

Debugging Dojo

Debugging JavaScript can be difficult. Dojo can come to the rescue with its own useful debugging facilities. To enable these facilities, set the Dojo `djconfig` configuration attribute `isDebug` to `true`.

The example textboxdebug.html shows how to turn on Dojo debugging. This example then deliberately causes an error—an attempt to access a nonexistent text box with the ID `"text2"`—so you can see how the Dojo debugging facilities take over.

To turn on debugging in Dojo:

1. Open your Web page, such as textboxdebug.html, in a text editor.

2. In the `<script>` element that loads dojo.js, assign the `djconfig` attribute the value `"isDebug:true, parseOnLoad:true"`.

3. Create a deliberate error in your code, such as having your code attempt to work with a nonexistent text box with the ID `"text2"`.

   Script 2.4 shows what your page should look like after you make the additions.

Script 2.4 Turning on debugging in Dojo.

```
1   <html>
2    <head>
3     <title>Debugging Dojo</title>
4      <link rel="stylesheet"
5       type="text/css"
6       href="http://o.aolcdn.com/
7       dojo/1.1/dojo/
8       resources/dojo.css" />
9
10     <link rel="stylesheet"
11      type="text/css"
12      href="http://o.aolcdn.com/dojo/
13      1.1/dijit/
14      themes/tundra/tundra.css" />
15
16     <script
17      djConfig="isDebug:true,
18        parseOnLoad:true"
19      type="text/javascript"
20      src="http://o.aolcdn.com/dojo/1.1/
21       dojo/dojo.xd.js">
22     </script>
23
24     <script type="text/javascript">
25       dojo.require("dojo.parser");
26       dojo.require("dijit.form.Button");
27       dojo.require("dijit.form.TextBox");
28
29       dojo.addOnLoad(function( ) {
30        dojo.connect(dijit.byId("button"),
31        "onClick", function(evt) {
32          dijit.byId("text2").setValue(
33          "Welcome to Dojo");
34        });
35       });
36     </script>
37    <head>
38
39    <body class="tundra">
40     <h1>Debugging Dojo</h1>
41      <br>
```

(script continues)

Script 2.4 *continued*

```
                         script
42        <button
43         id="button"
44         dojoType="dijit.form.Button">
45         Click me
46        </button>
47
48        <input id="text" type="text"
49         name="text"
50         maxlength="25"
51         dojoType="dijit.form.TextBox">
52        </input>
53        <br>
54      </body>
55    </html>
```

4. Save your file.

5. Navigate to your file in a browser. You should see a button and a text box.

6. Click the button. JavaScript will try to access the nonexistent text box, which makes Dojo cause an error and explain it to you as shown in **Figure 2.5**.

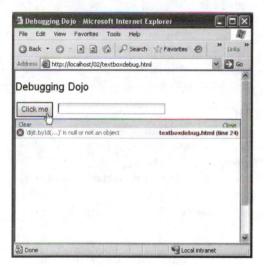

Figure 2.5 Displaying a debugging message.

Using ValidationTextBox

A big concern in JavaScript is validating what the user has entered before it is sent to the server. Dojo tackles this task with the ValidationTextBox, which lets you specify a regular expression that the entered text must match.

The next example, validationtextbox.html, uses Dojo validation with a simple regular expression that demands the user enter only alphabetical ("word") characters (that is, no characters such as?, &, and so on).

To turn on validation in Dojo:

1. Open your Web page, such as validationtextbox.html, in a text editor.

2. Add the statement dojo.require("dijit. form.ValidationTextBox"); to your code.

3. Create a new text box with the dojoType attribute set to "dijit.form.Validation TextBox", the promptMessage attribute (appears when the cursor enters the text box) set to "Enter only letters or numbers", the invalidMessage attribute (the error message) set to "Please use only letters or numbers", and the regExp attribute (contains the regular expression you want to match) set to "[\w]+" (for "words").

Script 2.5 shows what your page should look like after you make the additions.

Script 2.5 Turning on validation in Dojo.

```
1    <html>
2      <head>
3        <title>Using
4        ValidationTextBox</title>
5        <link rel="stylesheet"
6          type="text/css"
7          href="http://o.aolcdn.com/
8          dojo/1.1/dojo/
9          resources/dojo.css" />
10       <link rel="stylesheet"
11         type="text/css"
12         href="http://o.aolcdn.com/dojo/
13         1.1/dijit/
14         themes/tundra/tundra.css" />
15
16       <script
17         djConfig="parseOnLoad:true"
18         type="text/javascript"
19         src="http://o.aolcdn.com/dojo/1.1/
20           dojo/dojo.xd.js">
21       </script>
22
23       <script type="text/javascript">
24         dojo.require("dojo.parser");
25         dojo.require("dijit.form.Button");
26         dojo.require(
27           "dijit.form.ValidationTextBox");
28       </script>
29     <head>
30
31     <body class="tundra">
32       <h1>Using ValidationTextBox</h1>
33       <br>
34       <form id="registration_form"
35         method="POST"
36         action=
37         "http://localhost/02/reflect.php">
38
39         <button
40           id="button"
41           type="submit"
42           dojoType="dijit.form.Button">
```

(script continues)

Script 2.5 *continued*

```
43        Click me
44      </button>
45
46      <input id="text"
47        type="text"
48        name="text"
49        maxlength="25"
50        promptMessage=
51        "Enter only letters or numbers"
52        invalidMessage="Please use only
53        letters or numbers"
54        regExp="[\w]+"
55        dojoType=
56          "dijit.form.ValidationTextBox">
57      </input>
58    <br>
59    </form>
60    </body>
61 </html>
```

4. Save your file.

5. Navigate to your file in a browser. You should see a button and a text box.

6. Try entering an invalid character such as a question mark (?). An error message should appear (**Figure 2.6**).

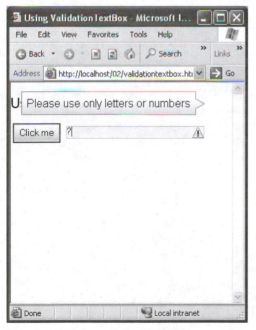

Figure 2.6 Validating user input in Dojo.

Using NumberTextBox

If you only want numbers in a certain range to be accepted in a text box, NumberTextBox is your ticket. It works much like ValidationTextBox, but you can also add min and max constraints to the allowed values. Like ValidationTextBox, NumberTextBox supports the invalidMessage and promptMessage attributes.

The example numbertextbox.html accepts only numbers in the format #.##, with a minimum possible value of 0.00 and a maximum of 9.99.

To perform numeric validation in Dojo:

1. Open your Web page, such as numbertextbox.html, in a text editor.

2. Add the statement dojo.require("dijit. form.NumberTextBox"); to your code.

3. Create a new text box with the dojoType attribute set to "dijit.form. NumberTextBox" and the constraints attribute set to "{pattern: '#.##', min: '0.00', max: '9.99'}".

   Script 2.6 shows what your page should look like after you make the additions.

Script 2.6 Performing numeric validation in Dojo.

```
1   <html>
2    <head>
3      <title>Using NumberTextBox</title>
4
5      <link rel="stylesheet"
6        type="text/css"
7        href="http://o.aolcdn.com/
8        dojo/1.1/dojo/
9        resources/dojo.css" />
10     <link rel="stylesheet"
11       type="text/css"
12       href="http://o.aolcdn.com/dojo/
13       1.1/dijit/
14       themes/tundra/tundra.css" />
15
16     <script
17       djConfig="parseOnLoad:true"
18       type="text/javascript"
19       src="http://o.aolcdn.com/dojo/1.1/
20        dojo/dojo.xd.js">
21     </script>
22
23     <script type="text/javascript">
24       dojo.require("dojo.parser");
25       dojo.require("dijit.form.Button");
26       dojo.require(
27        "dijit.form.NumberTextBox");
28
29       dojo.addOnLoad(function(){
30        dojo.connect(dijit.byId("button"),
31         "onClick", function(evt) {
32          alert("You entered: " +
33          dijit.byId("text").getValue());
34        });
35       });
36     </script>
37    <head>
38
39    <body class="tundra">
40     <h1>Using NumberTextBox</h1>
41     <br>
42     <button
```

(script continues)

Script 2.6 *continued*

```
                    script

43        id="button"
44        dojoType="dijit.form.Button">
45        Click me
46      </button>
47
48      <input id="text"
49        constraints="{pattern: '#.##', min:
50        '0.00', max: '9.99'}"
51        dojoType=
52        "dijit.form.NumberTextBox">
53      </input>
54      <br>
55    </body>
56  </html>
```

4. Save your file.

5. Navigate to your file in a browser. You should see a button and a text box.

6. Try entering an invalid, out-of-range number such as 10. An error message should appear (**Figure 2.7**).

✔ Tip

■ One annoying aspect of Validation-TextBox and NumberTextBox is that they display their error messages as the user is entering values, because partial values don't match the regular expression fully.

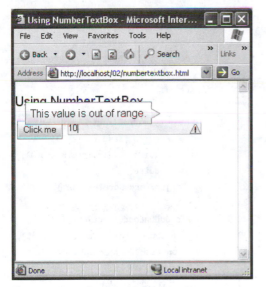

Figure 2.7 Accepting range-bound numbers.

Using DateTextBox

Dojo has a handy control that displays a calendar and lets the user select a date: DateTextBox. The calendar appears only when the text box has been clicked. In this control, the getValue method returns a JavaScript Date object; if you want the date as a string, you use the getDisplayedValue method.

The example datetextbox.html accepts dates from the user with a clickable Dojo calendar.

To let the user select dates from a clickable calendar:

1. Open your Web page, such as datetext-box.html, in a text editor.

2. Add the statement dojo.requiret("dijit.form.DateTextBox"); to your code.

3. Create a new text box with the dojoType attribute set to "dijit.form.DateTextBox" and connect a JavaScript function to a button in the page that displays the calendar's date in a JavaScript alert box using the getDisplayedValue method.

   Script 2.7 shows what your page should look like after you make the additions.

Script 2.7 Letting the user select dates from a clickable calendar.

```
1   <html>
2     <head>
3       <title>Using DateTextBox</title>
4
5       <link rel="stylesheet"
6         type="text/css"
7         href="http://o.aolcdn.com/
8         dojo/1.1/dojo/
9         resources/dojo.css" />
10      <link rel="stylesheet"
11        type="text/css"
12        href="http://o.aolcdn.com/dojo/
13        1.1/dijit/
14        themes/tundra/tundra.css" />
15
16      <script
17        djConfig="parseOnLoad:true"
18        type="text/javascript"
19        src="http://o.aolcdn.com/dojo/1.1/
20        dojo/dojo.xd.js">
21      </script>
22
23      <script type="text/javascript">
24        dojo.require("dojo.parser");
25        dojo.require("dijit.form.Button");
26        dojo.require(
27          "dijit.form.DateTextBox");
28
29        dojo.addOnLoad(function(){
30         dojo.connect(dijit.byId("button"),
31           "onClick", function(evt) {
32             alert("Date: " +
33             dijit.byId("date")
34           .getDisplayedValue());
35          });
36        });
37
38      </script>
39    <head>
40
41    <body class="tundra">
```

(script continues)

Script 2.7 *continued*

```
42      <h1>Using DateTextBox</h1>
43      <br>
44      <form>
45
46        <button
47          id="button"
48          dojoType="dijit.form.Button">
49          Click me
50        </button>
51
52        <input id="date"
53          type="text"
54          dojoType=
55            "dijit.form.DateTextBox">
56        </input>
57        <br>
58      </form>
59    </body>
60  </html>
```

4. Save your file.

5. Navigate to your file in a browser. You should see a button and a text box.

6. Click the text box to display the calendar (**Figure 2.8**).

7. Click a date in the calendar to select a date.

8. Click the button to display the selected date in an alert box (**Figure 2.9**).

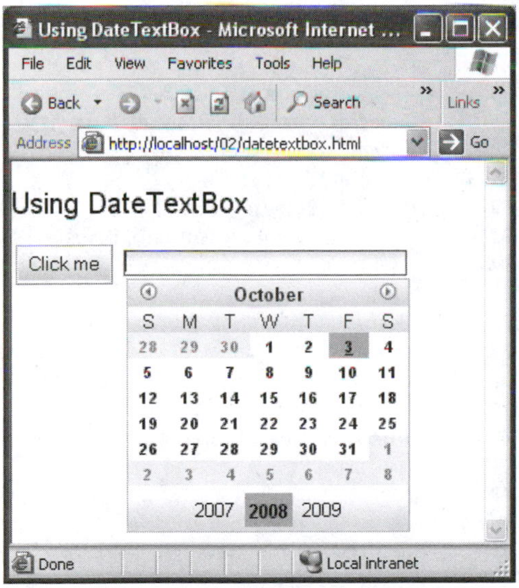

Figure 2.9 Displaying a date.

Figure 2.8 Displaying a calendar.

Using TimeTextBox

Dojo has a control that lets the user choose a time of day: TimeTextBox. This Dijit displays an accordion-like control when its text box is clicked. The control that appears lets the user click times in 15-minute increments, and the user can also edit the time in the text box for more precision. As with DateTextBox, the getValue method returns a JavaScript Date object; if you want the date as a string, you use the getDisplayedValue method.

The example timetextbox.html accepts times from the user with a clickable Dojo control.

To let the user select times from a clickable control:

1. Open your Web page, such as timetextbox.html, in a text editor.

2. Add the statement dojo.require("dijit. form.TimeTextBox"); to your code.

3. Create a new text box with the dojoType attribute set to "dijit.form.TimeTextBox" and connect a JavaScript function to a button in the page that displays the control's time using a JavaScript alert box and the getDisplayedValue method.

   Script 2.8 shows what your page should look like after you make the additions.

Script 2.8 Letting the user select times from a clickable control.

```
1    <html>
2      <head>
3        <title>Using TimeTextbox</title>
4        <link rel="stylesheet"
5          type="text/css"
6          href="http://o.aolcdn.com/
7          dojo/1.1/dojo/
8          resources/dojo.css" />
9        <link rel="stylesheet"
10         type="text/css"
11         href="http://o.aolcdn.com/dojo/
12         1.1/dijit/
13         themes/tundra/tundra.css" />
14
15       <script
16         djConfig="parseOnLoad:true"
17         type="text/javascript"
18         src="http://o.aolcdn.com/dojo/1.1/
19           dojo/dojo.xd.js">
20       </script>
21
22       <script type="text/javascript">
23         dojo.require("dojo.parser");
24         dojo.require("dijit.form.Button");
25         dojo.require(
26           "dijit.form.TimeTextBox");
27
28         dojo.addOnLoad(function(){
29          dojo.connect(dijit.byId("button"),
30          "onClick", function(evt) {
31            alert("Time: " +
32              dijit.byId("time")
33              .getDisplayedValue());
34          });
35         });
36       </script>
37     <head>
38
39     <body class="tundra">
40       <h1>Using TimeTextbox</h1>
41       <br>
42       <form>
43
44         <button
45           id="button"
46           dojoType="dijit.form.Button">
47           Click me
48         </button>
49
```

(script continues)

Script 2.8 *continued*

```
                    script
 50        <input id="time"
 51          type="text"
 52          dojoType=
 53            "dijit.form.TimeTextBox">
 54        </input>
 55      <br>
 56      </form>
 57    </body>
 58  </html>
```

4. Save your file.

5. Navigate to your file in a browser. You should see a button and a text box.

6. Click the text box to display the time control (**Figure 2.10**).

7. Click the time control to select a time.

8. Click the button to display the selected time in an alert box (**Figure 2.11**).

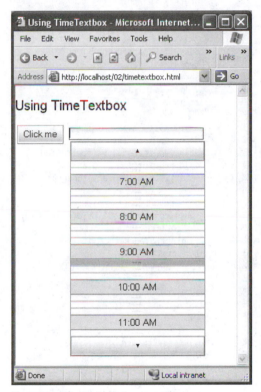

Figure 2.10 Displaying a time control.

Figure 2.11 Displaying a selected time.

Using NumberSpinner

Dojo also supports another variation on the standard text box: the NumberSpinner control. This control is like a text box, but it displays up and down arrows to let the user select numbers. You set the original value displayed with the value attribute, and you set the minimum and maximum allowable values with the min and max constraints.

The example numberspinner.html lets the user select numbers with a number spinner.

To let the user select numbers with a number spinner:

1. Open your Web page, such as numberspinner.html, in a text editor.

2. Add the statement dojo.require("dijit. form.NumberSpinner"); to your code.

3. Create a new text box with the dojoType attribute set to "dijit.form. NumberSpinner", the constraints attribute set to "{min:0, max:10000}", the value attribute set to "1000", and the ID attribute set to "number".

4. Connect a JavaScript function to a button in the page that displays the control's value using a JavaScript alert box and the getValue method.

   Script 2.9 shows what your page should look like after you make the additions.

Script 2.9 Letting the user select numbers with a number spinner.

```
1   <html>
2     <head>
3       <title>Using Number Spinner</title>
4       <link rel="stylesheet"
5         type="text/css"
6         href="http://o.aolcdn.com/
7         dojo/1.1/dojo/
8         resources/dojo.css" />
9       <link rel="stylesheet"
10        type="text/css"
11        href="http://o.aolcdn.com/dojo/
12        1.1/dijit/
13        themes/tundra/tundra.css" />
14      <script
15        djConfig="parseOnLoad:true"
16        type="text/javascript"
17        src="http://o.aolcdn.com/dojo/1.1/
18        dojo/dojo.xd.js">
19      </script>
20
21      <script type="text/javascript">
22        dojo.require("dojo.parser");
23        dojo.require("dijit.form.Button");
24        dojo.require(
25          "dijit.form.NumberSpinner");
26
27        dojo.addOnLoad(function( ){
28         dojo.connect(dijit.byId("button"),
29          "onClick", function(evt) {
30          alert("You selected: " +
31            dijit.byId(
32              "number").getValue());
33         });
34        });
35      </script>
36    <head>
37
38    <body class="tundra">
39      <h1>Using NumberSpinner</h1>
40      <br>
41      <input
42        dojoType="dijit.form.NumberSpinner"
43        constraints="{min:0, max:10000}"
44        value="1000"
45        id="number"
46      ></input>
47
48      <button
49        id="button"
50        dojoType="dijit.form.Button">
51        Click me
52      </button>
53    </body>
54  </html>
```

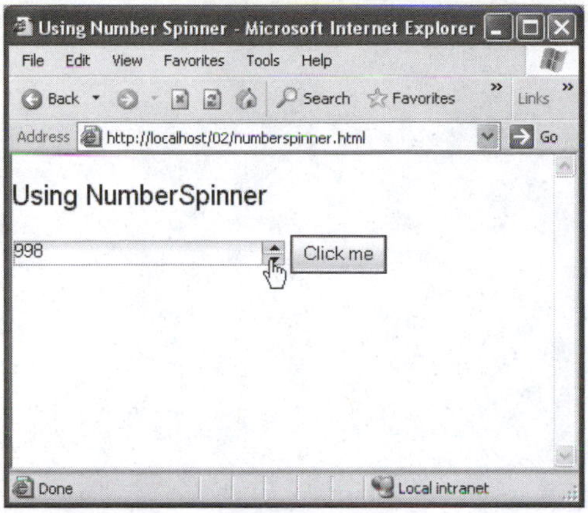

Figure 2.12 Displaying a number spinner.

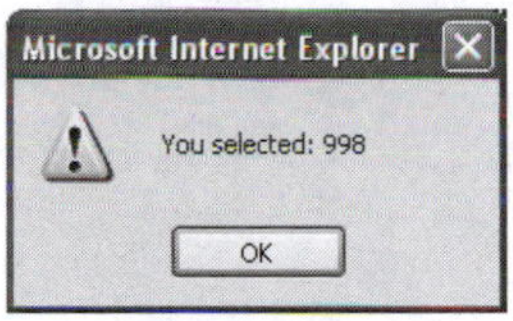

Figure 2.13 Displaying a selected number.

5. Save your file.

6. Navigate to your file in a browser. You should see a button and number spinner.

7. Click the number spinner to select a number (**Figure 2.12**).

8. Click the time control to select a number.

9. Click the button to display the selected number in an alert box (**Figure 2.13**).

FORM DIJITS: COMBO BOXES, TOGGLES, AND MORE

3

Dojo is packed with dozens of Dijits, and they're the draw that most often brings programmers to Dojo. In the previous chapter, we got started with Dojo form elements, but Dojo has plenty more to offer. In this chapter, we'll look at Dojo check boxes, radio buttons, combo boxes, toggle buttons, multiselect selection controls, sliders, drop-down menu buttons, and combo buttons.

Some of the Dojo form Dijits, such as check boxes and radio buttons, mimic standard HTML controls, and others, such as sliders and number spinners, have no counterparts in HTML. But all can be styled with Dojo styles, and you can use Dojo methods on them, such as `connect` and `byId`, as you'll see as we continue our guided tour of form Dijits.

Using CheckBox

The Dojo CheckBox Dijit is very like the HTML check box, except that you can use Dojo methods and styles on it. If you're using Dijits in a Web page and want to add check boxes, instead of using standard HTML check boxes and writing their code in a way that doesn't match the rest of the Dijits in your page, you can use Dijit check boxes.

Check boxes have an on/off setting you access with the Dijit property checked and a value (that is, text) that you access with getValue.

We'll explore an example here, checkbox.html.

To add Dijit check boxes:

1. Open your Web page in a text editor.

2. Add dojo.require("dijit.form. Button"); and dojo.require("dijit. form.CheckBox"); statements to your code.

3. Create a new Dijit check box with the value "yes" and the ID "check" and then add a button that displays the check box's value and checked status in alert boxes.

   Script 3.1 shows what your page should look like after you make the additions.

Script 3.1 Adding Dijit check boxes.

```
1   <html>
2     <head>
3       <title>Using CheckBox</title>
4       <link rel="stylesheet"
5         type="text/css"
6         href="http://o.aolcdn.com/
7         dojo/1.1/dojo/
8         resources/dojo.css" />
9       <link rel="stylesheet"
10        type="text/css"
11        href="http://o.aolcdn.com/dojo/
12        1.1/dijit/
13        themes/tundra/tundra.css" />
14      <script
15        djConfig="parseOnLoad:true"
16        type="text/javascript"
17        src="http://o.aolcdn.com/dojo/1.1/
18        dojo/dojo.xd.js">
19      </script>
20      <script type="text/javascript">
21        dojo.require("dojo.parser");
22        dojo.require("dijit.form.Button");
23        dojo.require("dijit.form.CheckBox");
24
25        dojo.addOnLoad(function( ){
26          dojo.connect(dijit.byId("button"),
27            "onClick", function(evt) {
28            alert("The check box is set to:
29            " + dijit.byId("check").
30            getValue());
31            if(dijit.byId("check")
32            .checked){
33            alert("The check box is
34            checked.");
35            }else{
36            alert("The check box is not
37            checked.");
38            }
39          });
40        });
41      </script>
42    <head>
```

(script continues)

Script 3.1 *continued*

```
43
44    <body class="tundra">
45      <h1>Using CheckBox</h1>
46      <br>
47      <input
48        dojoType="dijit.form.CheckBox"
49        value="Yes"
50        id="check"
51      ></input>
52      <button
53        id="button"
54        dojoType="dijit.form.Button">
55        Click me
56      </button>
57    </body>
58  </html>
```

4. Save your file.

5. Navigate to your file in a browser. You should see a button and a check box (**Figure 3.1**).

6. Check the check box and click the button.

   The value of the check box is displayed in an alert box (**Figure 3.2**).

7. Click OK to dismiss the alert with the check box's value.

   Another alert box appears, this one reporting the checked status of the check box (**Figure 3.3**).

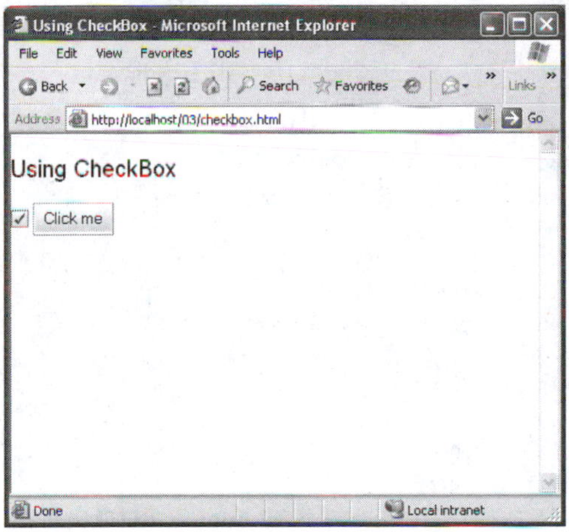

Figure 3.1 A Dijit check box.

Figure 3.2 The check box's value.

Figure 3.3 The check box's checked status.

USING CHECKBOX

Using RadioButton

Another Dijit that mirrors what's available in HTML is the RadioButton Dijit. It's just like its HTML counterpart, but again, if you're using other Dijits in your Web page, you probably don't want to drop back to HTML to add radio buttons. Radio buttons are descended from check boxes, so you require `dijit.form.CheckBox`, not `dijit.form.RadioButton` (which doesn't exist).

Here's an example, radiobutton.html, that shows how to use Dijit radio buttons.

To add Dijit radio buttons:

1. Open your Web page, such as checkbox.html, in a text editor.

2. Add `dojo.require("dijit.form.Button");` and `dojo.require("dijit.form.CheckBox");` statements to your code.

3. Add the question *Do you want cash back?* to the page and create two new Dijit radio buttons with the values "Yes" and "No". Then add a button that displays the first radio button's value and then the value of both radio buttons in alert boxes.

Script 3.2 shows what your page should look like after you make the additions.

Script 3.2 Adding Dijit radio buttons.

```
1    <html>
2      <head>
3        <title>Using Radio Buttons</title>
(4-18)   . . .
19       <script type="text/javascript">
20        dojo.require("dojo.parser");
21        dojo.require("dijit.form.Button");
22        dojo.require("dijit.form.CheckBox");
23
24        dojo.addOnLoad(function( ){
25         dojo.connect(dijit.byId(
26          "button"), "onClick",
27          function(evt) {
28          alert("The first radio button
29          is set to: " +
30          dijit.byId("radio1").getValue());
31          for
32          (i=0;i<document.forms[0]
33           .radios.length;i++) {
34         if (document.forms[0]
35          .radios[i].checked) {
36         alert("The radio buttons are
37          set to: " +
38          document.forms[0].radios[i]
39          .value);
40         }
41         }
42         });
43         });
44      </script>
45    <head>
46    <body class="tundra">
47      <h1>Using Radio Buttons</h1>
48      <br>
49      <form>
50      Do you want cash back?
51      <input
52        dojoType="dijit.form.RadioButton"
53        value="Yes"
54        id="radio1"
55        name="radios">
56        Yes</input>
57      <input
58        dojoType="dijit.form.RadioButton"
59        value="No"
60        id="radio2"
61        name="radios">
62        No</input>
(63-77)  . . .
78    </html>
```

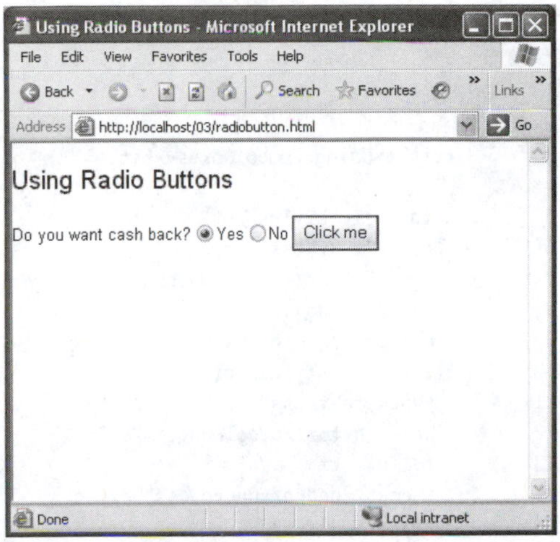

Figure 3.4 Dijit radio buttons.

Figure 3.5 The first radio button's value.

Figure 3.6 The selected radio buttons' value.

4. Save your file.

5. Navigate to your file in a browser. You should see a button and two radio buttons (**Figure 3.4**).

6. Check the first radio button and click the button.

   The value of the first radio button is displayed in an alert box (**Figure 3.5**).

✔ **Tip**

■ The value of the radio button is independent of whether or not it's selected—the value is the HTML attribute of the same name and does not indicate whether the radio button is selected.

7. Click OK to dismiss the alert box with the first radio button's value.

   Now you should see the value of the radio button that's selected (**Figure 3.6**).

USING RADIOBUTTON

41

Using ComboBox

Dojo also supports a combo box, which is a combination of a text box and a drop-down list.

This example, combobox.html, shows how to use Dijit combo boxes in a simple Web page that asks you to select a flavor of ice cream and reports your selection in an alert box, using the combo box's onChange event.

To add Dijit combo boxes:

1. Open your Web page, such as checkbox. html, in a text editor.

2. Add the dojo.require("dijit.form. ComboBox"); statement to your code.

3. Add the prompt *Select your ice cream:* to the page and create a new Dijit combo box with the values *Strawberry*, *Vanilla*, *Chocolate*, and *Pistachio*. Then connect a function to the combo box's onChange event to display the current selection (passed to the onChange event handler) in an alert box.

   Script 3.3 shows what your page should look like after you make the additions.

Script 3.3 Adding Dijit combo boxes.

```
1   <html>
2     <head>
3       <title>Using Combo Boxes</title>
4
5       <link rel="stylesheet"
6         type="text/css"
7         href="http://o.aolcdn.com/
8         dojo/1.1/dojo/
9         resources/dojo.css" />
10      <link rel="stylesheet"
11        type="text/css"
12        href="http://o.aolcdn.com/dojo/
13        1.1/dijit/
14        themes/tundra/tundra.css" />
15      <script
16        djConfig="parseOnLoad:true"
17        type="text/javascript"
18        src="http://o.aolcdn.com/dojo/1.1/
19          dojo/dojo.xd.js">
20      </script>
21
22      <script type="text/javascript">
23        dojo.require("dojo.parser");
24        dojo.require("dijit.form.ComboBox");
25
26      </script>
27    <head>
28
29    <body class="tundra">
30      <h1>Using Combo Boxes</h1>
31      <br>
32      Select your ice cream:
33      <br>
34      <select name="icecream"
35        dojoType="dijit.form.ComboBox"
36        autoComplete="true">
37        <option>Strawberry</option>
38        <option>Vanilla</option>
39        <option>Chocolate</option>
40        <option selected>
41          Pistachio
42        </option>
43        <script type="dojo/method"
44          event="onChange"
45          args="newValue">
46          alert("You selected: "
47          + newValue);
48        </script>
49      </select>
50    </body>
51  </html>
```

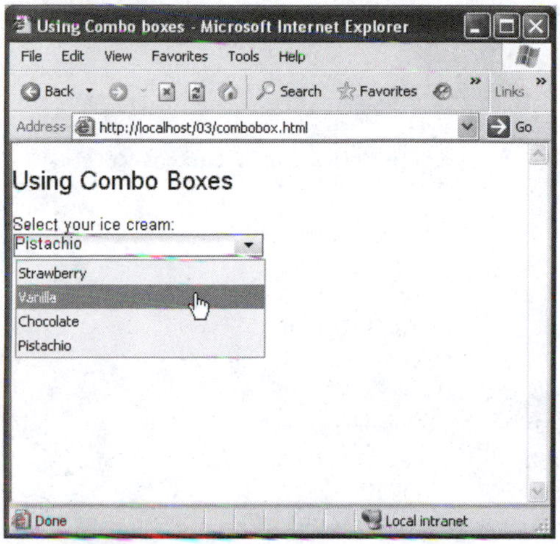

Figure 3.7 Dijit combo box.

Figure 3.8 The flavor you selected.

4. Save your file.

5. Navigate to your file in a browser. You should see a combo box with a menu of ice cream flavors (**Figure 3.7**).

6. Make a selection in the combo box.

   You should see an alert box indicating your selection (**Figure 3.8**).

Using ToggleButton

Toggle buttons have two states: clicked and unclicked. You can determine whether the button is clicked or unclicked with its `getValue` method or by looking at the true/false value passed to an `onChange` event handler. Toggle buttons are a kind of button, so you require `dijit.form.Button`.

This example, togglebutton.html, uses the toggle button's `onChange` event to display an alert box each time you click the button.

To add toggle buttons

1. Open your Web page, such as checkbox.html, in a text editor.

2. Add a `dojo.require("dijit.form.Button");` statement to your code.

3. Create a new toggle button with the `dojoType` attribute set to `"dijit.form.ToggleButton"` and connect its `onChange` event to a function that reports whether the button is clicked.

   Script 3.4 shows what your page should look like after you make the additions.

Script 3.4 Adding toggle buttons.

```
1    <html>
2      <head>
3        <title>Using Toggle Buttons</title>
4
5        <link rel="stylesheet"
6          type="text/css"
7          href="http://o.aolcdn.com/
8          dojo/1.1/dojo/
9          resources/dojo.css" />
10       <link rel="stylesheet"
11         type="text/css"
12         href="http://o.aolcdn.com/dojo/
13         1.1/dijit/
14         themes/tundra/tundra.css" />
15       <script
16         djConfig="parseOnLoad:true"
17         type="text/javascript"
18         src="http://o.aolcdn.com/dojo/1.1/
19           dojo/dojo.xd.js">
20       </script>
21
22       <script type="text/javascript">
23         dojo.require("dojo.parser");
24         dojo.require("dijit.form.Button");
25
26       </script>
27     <head>
28
29     <body class="tundra">
30       <h1>Using Toggle Buttons</h1>
31       <br>
32       <button
33         dojoType="dijit.form.ToggleButton">
34         <script type="dojo/method"
35         event="onChange" args="newValue">
36          if(newValue){
37            alert("The button is
38              clicked.");
39          }else{
40            alert("The button is
41              unclicked.");
42          }
43         </script>
44       Click me
45       </button>
46     </body>
47   </html>
```

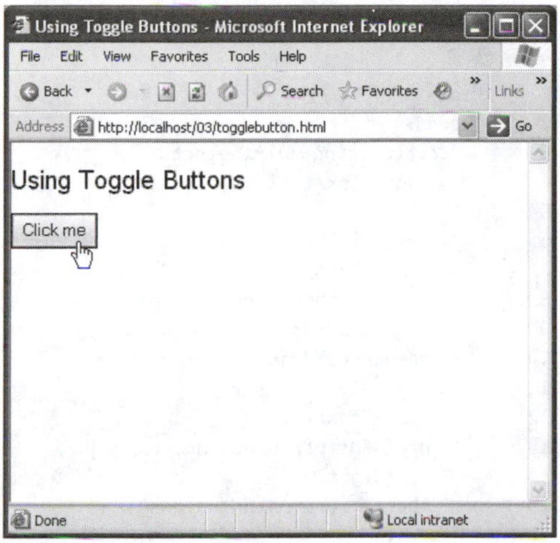

Figure 3.9 A Dijit toggle button.

Figure 3.10 Indicating that the toggle button is clicked.

Figure 3.11 Indicating that the toggle button is unclicked.

4. Save your file.

5. Navigate to your file in a browser. You should see the toggle button (**Figure 3.9**).

6. Click the toggle button.

   An alert box indicates that the button is clicked (**Figure 3.10**).

7. Click OK to dismiss the alert box. Then click the toggle button again.

   Now an alert box indicates that the button is unclicked (**Figure 3.11**).

Using MultiSelect

You can use Dijit multiselect selection controls to display drop-down (or stay-open) lists of clickable items the user can select.

This example, multiselect.html, asks where the user has lived, presenting a list of states to choose from. When the user makes a selection, which can consist of multiple states, an alert box displays a comma-separated list of the selected states' postal abbreviations (NY, CA, and so on).

To add multiselect selection controls:

1. Open your Web page, such as checkbox. html, in a text editor.

2. Add a `dojo.require("dijit.form. MultiSelect");` statement to your code.

3. Create a new `<select>` control with the `dojoType` attribute set to `"dijit.form. MultiSelect"` and connect its `onChange` event to a function that uses an alert box to display the value passed to the function.

   The value passed to the `onChange` event handler will be a comma-separated list of values from the MultiSelect Dijit.

   Script 3.5 shows what your page should look like after you make the additions.

Script 3.5 Adding multiselect selection controls.

```
1    <html>
2      <head>
3        <title>Using MultiSelect
4        Controls</title>
5
6        <link rel="stylesheet"
7        type="text/css"
8        href="http://o.aolcdn.com/
9        dojo/1.1/dojo/
10       resources/dojo.css" />
11       <link rel="stylesheet"
12       type="text/css"
13       href="http://o.aolcdn.com/dojo/
14       1.1/dijit/
15       themes/tundra/tundra.css" />
16       <script
17       djConfig="parseOnLoad:true"
18       type="text/javascript"
19       src="http://o.aolcdn.com/dojo/1.1/
20         dojo/dojo.xd.js">
21       </script>
22
23       <script type="text/javascript">
24         dojo.require("dojo.parser");
25         dojo.require("dijit.form
26           .MultiSelect");
27
28       </script>
29     <head>
30
31     <body class="tundra">
32       <h1>Using MultiSelect Controls</h1>
33       <br>
34       Where have you lived?
35       <br>
36       <select multiple="true"
37       dojoType="dijit.form.MultiSelect">
38         <option value="NY"
39           selected="true">New York</option>
40         <option value="MA">
41           Massachusetts</option>
42         <option value="CA">
43           California</option>
44         <option value="AK">Alaska</option>
45         <option value="PA">
46           Pennsylvania</option>
47         <script type="dojo/method"
48           event="onChange" args="newValue">
49           alert("You have lived in " +
50             newValue);
51         </script>
52       </select>
53     </body>
54   </html>
```

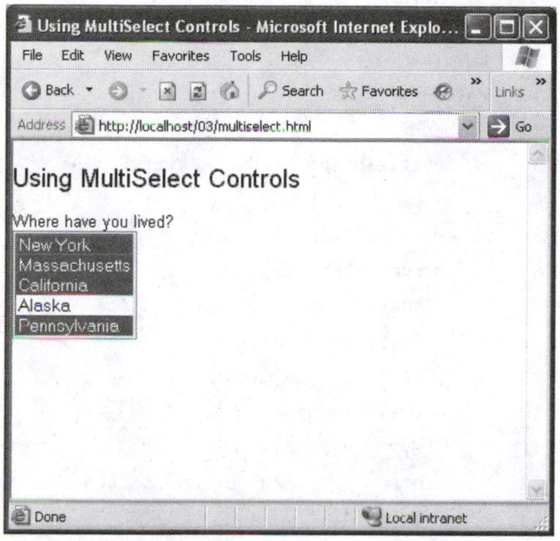

Figure 3.12 A multiselect control.

Figure 3.13 Selecting states in the multiselect control.

4. Save your file.

5. Navigate to your file in a browser. You should see a multiselect list (**Figure 3.12**).

6. Select several states. An alert box appears to let you know which ones you've selected (**Figure 3.13**).

Chapter 3

Using Slider

Here's a cool Dijit: Slider. This Dijit displays a control like the slider on a stereo, and it has no counterpart among the standard HTML controls. You drag the slider box to the location you want, and in code, you can determine the slider's position with the `getValue` method or by examining the value passed to the `onChange` event handler. Sliders come in two varieties: vertical and horizontal.

This example, sliders.html, displays both vertical and horizontal sliders and displays the new setting of each slider in an alert box when you drag the slider box.

To add sliders:

1. Open your Web page, such as checkbox.html, in a text editor.

2. Add a `dojo.require("dijit.form.SLider");` statement to your code.

3. To create the sliders and make them active, create two new `<div>` elements with `dojoType` `dijit.form.VerticalSlider` and `dijit.form.HorizontalSlider`, and set the `min` and `max` attributes to establish the sliders' ranges. Set `value` attributes to set the current values, and set the dimensions of the sliders with `style` attributes.

   Script 3.6 shows what your page should look like after you make the additions.

Script 3.6 Adding sliders.

```
1   <html>
2     <head>
3       <title>Using Sliders</title>
4
5       <link rel="stylesheet"
6         type="text/css"
7         href="http://o.aolcdn.com/
8         dojo/1.1/dojo/
9         resources/dojo.css" />
10      <link rel="stylesheet"
11        type="text/css"
12        href="http://o.aolcdn.com/dojo/
13        1.1/dijit/
14        themes/tundra/tundra.css" />
15      <script
16        djConfig="parseOnLoad:true"
17        type="text/javascript"
18        src="http://o.aolcdn.com/dojo/1.1/
19          dojo/dojo.xd.js">
20      </script>
21
22      <script type="text/javascript">
23        dojo.require("dojo.parser");
24        dojo.require("dijit.form.Slider");
25
26      </script>
27    <head>
28
29    <body class="tundra">
30      <h1>Using Sliders</h1>
31      <br>
32      <div
33        dojoType="dijit.form.VerticalSlider"
34        value="100"
35        maximum="200"
36        minimum="0"
37        style="width:100px; height: 200px;">
38
39        <script type="dojo/method"
40          event="onChange" args="newValue">
41          alert("You selected: " + newValue);
42        </script>
43      </div>
44      <div
```

(script continues)

Script 3.6 *continued*

```
45        dojoType=
46        "dijit.form.HorizontalSlider"
47        value="50"
48        maximum="100"
49        minimum="0"
50        style="width:200px; height: 20px;">
51        <script type="dojo/method"
52        event="onChange" args="newValue">
53        alert("You selected: " + newValue);
54        </script>
55      </dtiv>
56    </body>
57  </html>
```

4. Save your file.

5. Navigate to your file in a browser. You should see two sliders (**Figure 3.14**).

6. Drag the slider box of a slider to a new position. You should see an alert box displaying the new value (**Figure 3.15**).

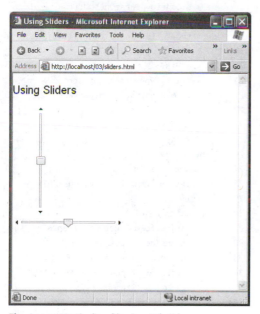

Figure 3.14 Vertical and horizontal sliders.

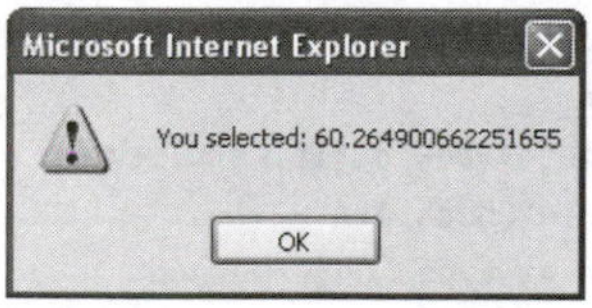

Figure 3.15 A new slider value.

Using DropDownButton

Drop-down buttons are considered form Dijits in Dojo, but they're actually a little more advanced and should be considered application Dijits because they enclose menus (which are application Dijits). A drop-down button displays a down arrow and, when the arrow button is clicked, displays a drop-down menu you can select from.

This example, dropdownbutton.html, displays ice cream flavors in a menu, and when the user selects one, that flavor is displayed in an alert box.

✔ Tip

■ We're getting a little ahead of ourselves by working with menus here. For more on menus, see Chapter 5, "Application Dijits: Tool Tips and More."

To add drop-down buttons:

1. Open your Web page, such as checkbox. html, in a text editor.

2. Add dojo.require statements for dijit. form.Button and dijit.Menu to your code.

3. To create the drop-down button, create a new button with the dojoType attribute set to dijit.form.DropDownButton and enclose a menu (see Chapter 5 for details) created from <div> elements with dojoType attributes set to dijit.Menu and dijit.MenuItem.

   Script 3.7 shows what your page should look like after you make the additions.

Script 3.7 Adding drop-down buttons.

```
1   <html>
2     <head>
3       <title>Using Drop Down
4         Buttons</title>
5       <link rel="stylesheet"
6         type="text/css"
7         href="http://o.aolcdn.com/
8         dojo/1.1/dojo/
9         resources/dojo.css" />
10      <link rel="stylesheet"
11        type="text/css"
12        href="http://o.aolcdn.com/dojo/
13        1.1/dijit/
14        themes/tundra/tundra.css" />
15      <script
16        djConfig="parseOnLoad:true"
17        type="text/javascript"
18        src="http://o.aolcdn.com/dojo/1.1/
19          dojo/dojo.xd.js">
20      </script>
21      <script type="text/javascript">
22        dojo.require("dojo.parser");
23        dojo.require("dijit.form.Button");
24        dojo.require("dijit.Menu");
25      </script>
26    <head>
27    <body class="tundra">
28      <h1>Using Drop Down Buttons</h1>
29      <br>
30      <button dojoType=
31        "dijit.form.DropDownButton">
32        <span>Ice cream</span>
33        <div dojoType="dijit.Menu">
34          <div dojoType="dijit.MenuItem"
35            label="Strawberry">
36            <script type="dojo/method"
37              event="onClick" args="evt">
38              alert("you clicked
39                Strawberry");
40            </script>
41          </div>
42          <div dojoType="dijit.MenuItem"
43            label="Chocolate">
44            <script type="dojo/method"
45              event="onClick" args="evt">
```

(script continues)

Script 3.7 *continued*

```
        script
46              alert("you clicked
47                Chocolate");
48              </script>
49          </div>
50          <div dojoType="dijit.MenuItem"
51            label="Vanilla">
52            <script type="dojo/method"
53              event="onClick" args="evt">
54                alert("you clicked
55                  Vanilla");
56            </script>
57          </div>
58        </div>
59      </button>
60    </body>
61  </html>
```

4. Save your file.

5. Navigate to your file. You should see a drop-down button (**Figure 3.16**).

6. Select an item in the menu. That item should appear in an alert box (**Figure 3.17**).

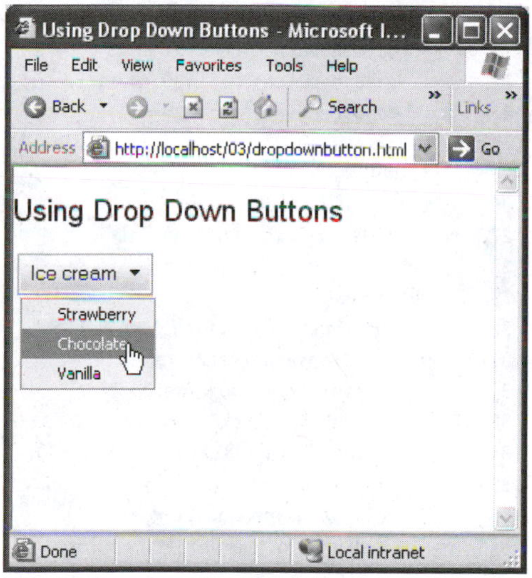

Figure 3.16 A drop-down button.

Figure 3.17 Selecting an item.

Using ComboButton

A combo button is a lot like a drop-down button combined with a standard button Dijit—and in fact, that's exactly what it is. You can click either the button or the down arrow (which opens the drop-down menu).

This example, combobutton.html, shows how to use combo buttons.

✔ Tip

■ As with drop-down buttons, we're getting a bit ahead of ourselves, because combo buttons require the use of menus. See Chapter 5 for details about menus.

To add combo buttons:

1. Open your Web page, such as checkbox. html, in a text editor.

2. Add `dojo.require` statements for `dijit.form.Button` and `dijit.Menu` to your code.

3. To create the combo button, create a new button with the `dojoType` attribute set to `dijit.form.DropDownButton` and enclose a menu (see Chapter 5 details) created from `<div>` elements with `dojoType` attributes set to `dijit.Menu` and `dijit.MenuItem`.

   Script 3.8 shows what your page should look like after you make the additions.

Script 3.8 Adding combo buttons.

```
1    <html>
2      <head>
3        <title>Using Combo Buttons</title>
4        <link rel="stylesheet"
5          type="text/css"
6          href="http://o.aolcdn.com/
7          dojo/1.1/dojo/
8          resources/dojo.css" />
9        <link rel="stylesheet"
10         type="text/css"
11         href="http://o.aolcdn.com/dojo/
12         1.1/dijit/
13         themes/tundra/tundra.css" />
14       <script
15         djConfig="parseOnLoad:true"
16         type="text/javascript"
17         src="http://o.aolcdn.com/dojo/1.1/
18           dojo/dojo.xd.js">
19       </script>
20       <script type="text/javascript">
21         dojo.require("dojo.parser");
22         dojo.require("dijit.form.Button");
23         dojo.require("dijit.Menu");
24       </script>
25     <head>
26     <body class="tundra">
27       <h1>Using Combo Buttons</h1>
28       <br>
29       <button
30         dojoType="dijit.form.ComboButton">
31         <span>Vegetables</span>
32         <script type="dojo/method"
33           event="onClick" args="evt">
34           alert("You clicked the button");
35         </script>
36         <div dojoType="dijit.Menu">
37           <div dojoType="dijit.MenuItem"
38             label="Broccoli">
39             <script type="dojo/method"
40             event="onClick" args="evt">
41               alert("You clicked
42                 Brocolli");
43             </script>
44           </div>
45           <div dojoType="dijit.MenuItem"
46             label="Spinach">
47             <script type="dojo/method"
```

(script continues)

Script 3.8 *continued*

```
script
48            event="onClick" args="evt">
49              alert("You clicked Spinach");
50            </script>
51          </div>
52          <div dojoType="dijit.MenuItem"
53            label="Peas">
54            <script type="dojo/method"
55            event="onClick" args="evt">
56              alert("You clicked Peas");
57            </script>
58          </div>
59        </div>
60      </button>
61    </body>
62  </html>
```

4. Save your file.

5. Navigate to your file. You should see a combo button (**Figure 3.18**).

6. Click the down arrow button (not a menu item). That should display an alert box (**Figure 3.19**).

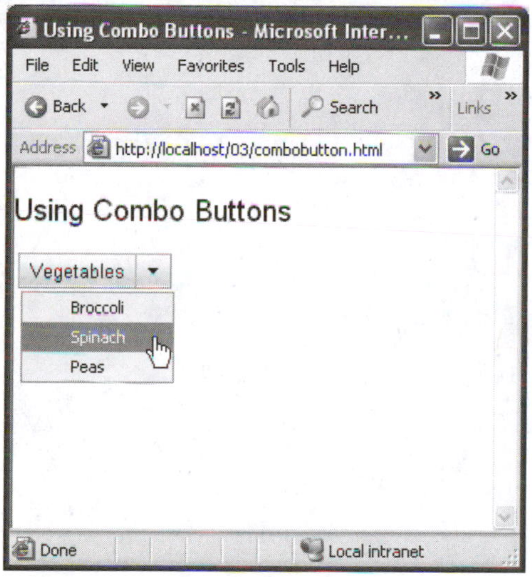

Figure 3.18 A combo button.

Figure 3.19 Clicking the combo button's button.

LAYOUT DIJITS

One of Dojo's specialties is layout Dijits. Layout Dijits let you arrange your other Dijits on a Web page, displaying them, for example, in tabbed pages. Because space is at a premium in browsers, tabs are very useful, especially if you have lots of controls to display, so you don't have to crowd them in.

Dojo also offers stack container Dijits, which lay out Dijits in a stack, with buttons to move through the stack. Click a button, and you're looking at the next page in the stack. Stack containers also help save space, but tab containers are more commonly understood by users.

A novel Dijit that Dojo offers is the accordion container, which presents the user with a set of labels arranged one next to the other. Clicking a label makes that accordion pleat open, revealing the controls it contains. The accordion layout Dijit is famous and has long been a hallmark of Dojo—in fact, some programmers think of the accordion container almost exclusively when they think of Dojo.

In this chapter, we'll explore these various types of Dijits.

Using ContentPane

The ContentPane Dijit is the Dijit that you use as a single page in a layout Dijit. For example, a tabbed container with six pages usually uses six content panes. You use the ContentPane Dijit to display each page of Dijits that you store in a layout container.

ContentPane Dijits are usually created from <div> elements with the dojotType attribute set to dijit.layout.ContentPane. Because a ContentPane Dijit is built from <div> elements, you can use a style attribute to arrange the Dijits in a content pane as you like.

The example here, contentpane.html, creates a content page and displays the text "This is a content pane." Because content panes are usually based on <div> elements, nothing special would appear in the Web page—just the text. To spiff things up a little, we'll also draw a dotted border around the content pane.

To create a content pane:

1. Open your Web page in a text editor.

2. Add a dojo.require("dijit.layout.ContentPane"); statement to your code.

3. Create a new <div> element with a border (use the style attribute to create the border) and set the <div> element's dojoType attribute to dijit.layout.ContentPane. Enclose some text in the <div> element.

   Script 4.1 shows what your page should look like after you make the additions.

Script 4.1 Creating a content pane.

```
1   <html>
2     <head>
3       <title>Using Content Panes</title>
4
5       <link rel="stylesheet"
6         type="text/css"
7         href="http://o.aolcdn.com/
8         dojo/1.1/dojo/
9         resources/dojo.css" />
10
11      <link rel="stylesheet"
12        type="text/css"
13        href="http://o.aolcdn.com/dojo/
14        1.1/dijit/
15        themes/tundra/tundra.css" />
16
17      <script
18        djConfig="parseOnLoad:true"
19        type="text/javascript"
20        src="http://o.aolcdn.com/dojo/1.1/
21          dojo/dojo.xd.js">
22      </script>
23
24      <script type="text/javascript">
25        dojo.require(
26        "dijit.layout.ContentPane");
27      </script>
28    </head>
29
30    <body class="tundra">
31      <h1>Using Content Panes</h1>
32      <br>
33      <div
34        dojoType=
35        "dijit.layout.ContentPane"
36        style=
37        "border: .2em dotted #900;">
38        This is a content pane.
39      </div>
40    </body>
41  </html>
```

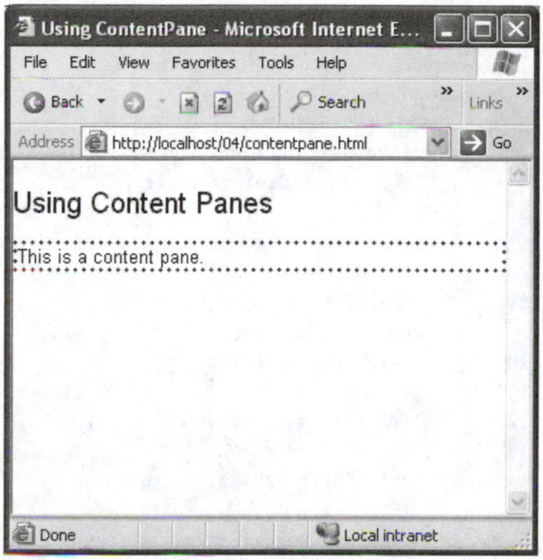

Figure 4.1 A Dijit content pane.

4. Save your file.

5. Navigate to your file in a browser. You should see the content pane, showing text and a dotted border (**Figure 4.1**).

✔ Tip

■ You can position Dijits in content panes using CSS positioning. Set the position style to `relative` and then use the `left` and `top` style properties to place items where you want them. See the next task for details.

Adding Dijits to a Content Pane

When you use a Dijit layout container, you place your Dijits in a content pane, where you can arrange them.

One way to arrange them is to use CSS positioning. Fundamentally, you can treat a content pane as a `<div>` element when placing other Dijits in it. You use relative positioning to position your Dijits with respect to the content pane.

The example contentpanetextbox.html shows how to add two text box Dijits to a content pane and arrange them.

To add Dijits to a content pane:

1. Open your Web page in a text editor.

2. Add `dojo.require("dijit.layout.ContentPane");` and `dojo.require("dijit.form.TextBox");` statements to your code.

3. Create a new `<div>` element with a border and set the `<div>` element's `dojoType` attribute to `dijit.layout.ContentPane`. Enclose two text box Dijits in the `<div>` element, using relative positioning to arrange them where you want in the content pane.

   Script 4.2 shows what your page should look like after you make the additions.

Script 4.2 Adding Dijits to a content pane.

```
1  <html>
2    <head>
3      <title>Using Content Panes
4      with Other Dijits</title>
5
6      <link rel="stylesheet"
7      type="text/css"
8      href="http://o.aolcdn.com/
9      dojo/1.1/dojo/
10     resources/dojo.css" />
11
12     <link rel="stylesheet"
13     type="text/css"
14     href="http://o.aolcdn.com/dojo/
15     1.1/dijit/
16     themes/tundra/tundra.css" />
17
18     <script
19     djConfig="parseOnLoad:true"
20     type="text/javascript"
21     src="http://o.aolcdn.com/dojo/1.1/
22     dojo/dojo.xd.js">
23     </script>
24
25     <script type="text/javascript">
26       dojo.require(
27       "dijit.layout.ContentPane");
28       dojo.require(
29       "dijit.form.TextBox");
30     </script>
31   </head>
32
33   <body class="tundra">
34     <h1>Using Content Panes with Other
35     Dijits</h1>
36       <br>
37       <div dojoType=
38       "dijit.layout.ContentPane"
39       style="border: .2em dotted #900;
40       height : 200px; width : 200px">
41         <input type="text"
42         dojoType="dijit.form.TextBox"
43         style="position:relative; top :
44         50px; left:50px">
45       <input type="text"
46       dojoType="dijit.form.TextBox"
47       style="position:relative; top :
48       80px; left:30px">
49     </div>
50   </body>
51 </html>
```

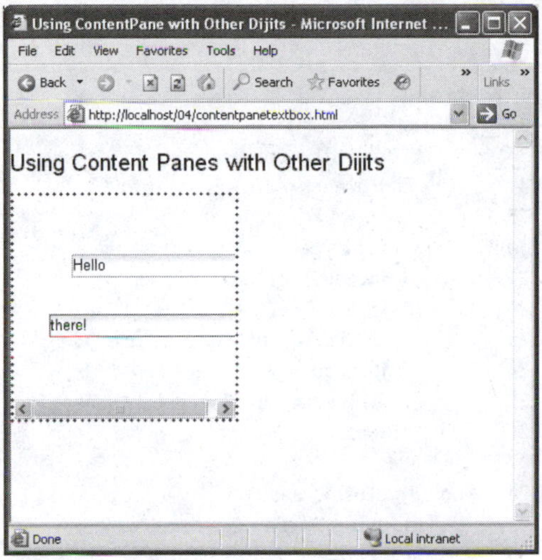

Figure 4.2 A content pane with two text boxes.

4. Save your file.

5. Navigate to your file in a browser. You should see two text boxes in a content pane with a dotted border (**Figure 4.2**).

6. Type something in the text boxes to confirm that they're functional, as shown in Figure 4.2.

Now that you have content panes down, you can start using them in layout containers.

Using BorderContainer

One of the most popular layout containers is the BorderContainer Dijit. This layout container lets you arrange content panes inside a common border by assigning values to their region attributes: "top", "bottom", "left", "right", and "center".

You can also allow the user to resize a content pane with the mouse by setting the content pane's splitter attribute to "true".

The example bordercontainer.html uses three content panes.

To add border containers:

1. Open your Web page in a text editor.

2. Add dojo.require("dijit.layout. ContentPane"); and dojo.require ("dijit.form.BorderContainer"); statements to your code.

3. To draw a border container with three content panes, create a new border container using a <div> element with its dojoType attribute set to dijit.form. BorderContainer and place three content panes inside it, with their region attributes set to "top", "center", and "bottom". Set the top and bottom content panes' splitter attributes to "true".

   Script 4.3 shows what your page should look like after you make the additions.

Script 4.3 Adding border containers.

```
1   <html>
2     <head>
3       <title>Using Border
4       Containers</title>
(5-19) . . .
20      <script type="text/javascript">
21        dojo.require("dojo.parser");
22        dojo.require(
23          "dijit.layout.ContentPane");
24        dojo.require(
25          "dijit.layout.BorderContainer");
26      </script>
27    </head>
28    <body class="tundra">
29      <h1>Using Border Containers</h1>
30      <br>
31      <div
32      dojoType=
33        "dijit.layout.BorderContainer"
34      style=
35        "height:100px;width:150px;
36        border:solid 2px;">
37        <div
38        dojoType=
39        "dijit.layout.ContentPane"
40        region="top"
41        style="background-color:pink;
42          height:30px;" splitter="true"
43          minSize="10" maxSize="800">
44          Top region
45        </div>
46        <div
47        dojoType=
48        "dijit.layout.ContentPane"
49        region="center">
50          Center region
51        </div>
52        <div
53        dojoType=
54        "dijit.layout.ContentPane"
55        region="bottom"
56        style="background-color:cyan;
57        height:30px;"
58        splitter="true"
59          minSize="10" maxSize="800">
60          Bottom region
61        </div>
62      </div>
63    </body>
64  </html>
```

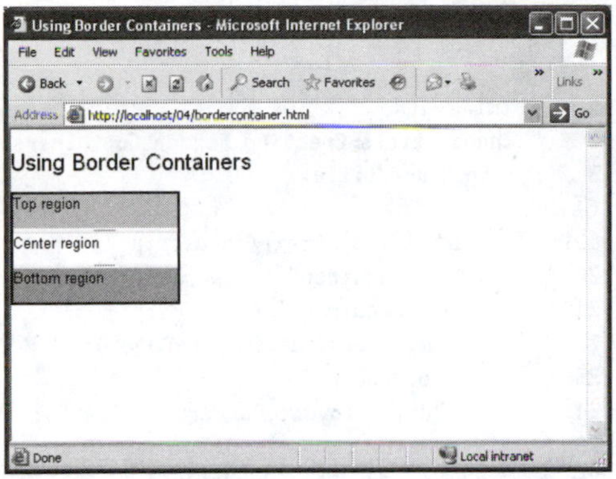

Figure 4.3 A border container with three content panes.

4. Save your file.

5. Navigate to your file in a browser. You should see a border container with three content panes (**Figure 4.3**).

You can resize the top and bottom content panes with the mouse. The cursor changes to a double-headed arrow for resizing.

Creating BorderContainer Dijits in Code

You can also create layout containers in code, not just markup as in the previous task. You'll do this in the next example, bordercontainerprogram.html.

To create a border container in code:

1. Open your Web page in a text editor.

2. Add dojo.require("dijit.layout. ContentPane"); and dojo.require ("dijit.form.BorderContainer"); statements to your code.

3. Create a new border container and three content panes in code; then call the container's startup method and the addChild method to add the content panes.

   Script 4.4 shows what your page should look like after you make the additions.

Script 4.4 Creating a border container in code.

```
1    <html>
2      <head><title>Creating Border Containers
3      in Code</title>
(4-18)  . . .
19     <script type="text/javascript">
20       dojo.require("dojo.parser");
21       dojo.require(
22         "dijit.layout.ContentPane");
23       dojo.require(
24         "dijit.layout.BorderContainer");
25
26       dojo.addOnLoad(function() {
27         var container = new
28         dijit.layout.BorderContainer(
29           {style: "height:100px;
30           width:150px;border:solid 2px"},
31           "container"
32         );
33         var div1 =
34         document.createElement("div");
35         div1.appendChild(document
36         .createTextNode("Top region"));
37         var div2 =
38         document.createElement("div");
39         div2.appendChild(document
40         .createTextNode("Center
41         region"));
42         var div3 =
43         document.createElement("div");
44         div3.appendChild(document
45         .createTextNode("Bottom
46         region"));
47         var top = new
48         dijit.layout.ContentPane(
49           {
50             region: "top",
51             style: "background-
52               color:pink;height:30px;",
53             splitter: true,
54             minSize : 10,
55             maxSize : 80
56           },
57           div1
58         );
59         var center = new
60           dijit.layout.ContentPane(
61           {
62             region: "center"
63           },
```

(script continues)

Script 4.4 *continued*

```
64        div2
65        );
66        var bottom = new
67          dijit.layout.ContentPane(
68          {
69            region: "bottom",
70            style: "background-color:cyan;
71              height:30px",
72            splitter: true
73          },
74          div3
75          );
76          container.startup();
77          container.addChild(top);
78          container.addChild(center);
79         container.addChild(bottom);
80        });
81      </script>
82    <head>
83    <body class="tundra">
84    <h1>Creating Border Containers in
85      Code</h1>
86    <br>
87    <div id="container">
88    </div>
89    </body>
90  </html>
```

4. Save your file.

5. Navigate to your file in a browser. You should see a new border container (**Figure** 4.4).

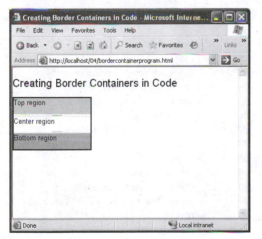

Figure 4.4 A border container created in code.

Using StackContainer

The stack container lets you stack pages (that is, content panes) on top of each other.

The next example, stackcontainer.html, creates a stack of four pages that list personnel at an imaginary company.

To add stack containers:

1. Open your Web page in a text editor.

2. Add dojo.require("dijit.layout. ContentPane"); and dojo.require ("dijit.form.StackContainer"); statements to your code.

3. Create a new stack container by setting a `<div>` element's dojoType attribute to dijit.form.StackContainer and enclose four content panes. Add two buttons that call the container's forward and back methods to navigate through the stack.

   Script 4.5 shows what your page should look like after you make the additions.

Script 4.5 Adding stack containers.

```
1   <html>
2     <head>
3       <title>Using Stack Containers</title>
4       <link rel="stylesheet"
5         type="text/css"
6         href="http://o.aolcdn.com/
7         dojo/1.1/dojo/
8         resources/dojo.css" />
9       <link rel="stylesheet"
10        type="text/css"
11        href="http://o.aolcdn.com/dojo/
12        1.1/dijit/
13        themes/tundra/tundra.css" />
14      <script
15        djConfig="parseOnLoad:true"
16        type="text/javascript"
17        src="http://o.aolcdn.com/dojo/1.1/
18          dojo/dojo.xd.js">
19      </script>
20      <script type="text/javascript">
21        dojo.require("dojo.parser");
22        dojo.require(
23          "dijit.layout.ContentPane");
24        dojo.require(
25          "dijit.layout.StackContainer");
26      </script>
27    </head>
28    <body class="tundra">
29      <h1>Using Stack Containers</h1>
30      <br>
31      <div id="stack"
32        dojoType=
33        "dijit.layout.StackContainer"
34        style="width:150px; height:75px;
35        margin:5px; border:solid 1px;">
36        <div dojoType=
37          "dijit.layout.ContentPane">
38          <b>Ralph Kramden</b><br>CEO
39        </div>
40        <div dojoType=
41          "dijit.layout.ContentPane">
42          <b>Ed Norton</b><br>VP Operations
43        </div>
44        <div dojoType=
45          "dijit.layout.ContentPane">
46          Alice Kramden<br>VP Marketing
47        </div>
```

(script continues)

Script 4.5 *continued*

```
48        <div dojoType=
49          "dijit.layout.ContentPane">
50          Trixie Norton<br>Treasurer
51        </div>
52      </div>
53      <button dojoType=
54        "dijit.form.Button">&lt;
55        <script type="dojo/method"
56          event="onClick" args="evt">
57          dijit.byId("stack").back( );
58        </script>
59      </button>
60      <button dojoType=
61        "dijit.form.Button">&gt;
62        <script type="dojo/method"
63          event="onClick" args="evt">
64          dijit.byId("stack").forward( );
65        </script>
66      </button>
67    </body>
68  </html>
```

4. Save your file.

5. Navigate to your file in a browser. You should see a stack container and two buttons (**Figure 4.5**).

6. Click the buttons to navigate from page to page (**Figure 4.6**).

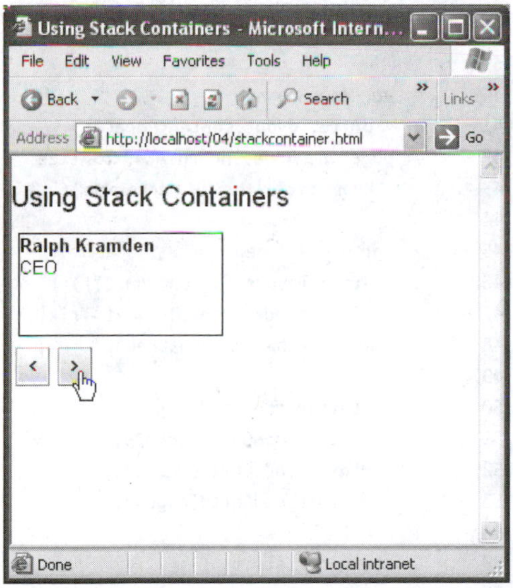

Figure 4.5 A stack container.

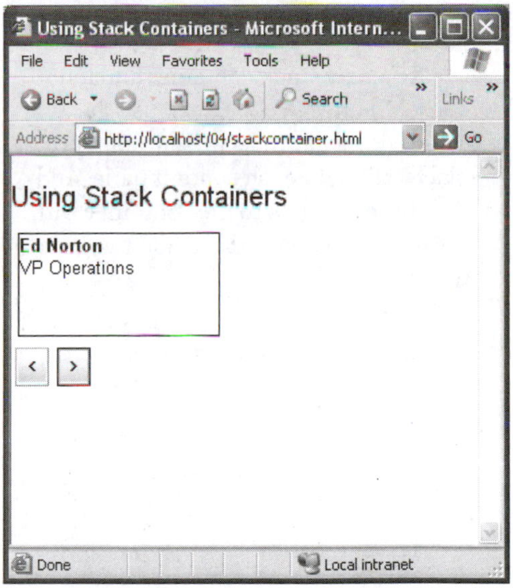

Figure 4.6 A new page in a stack container.

Creating StackContainer Dijits in Code

You can also create stack containers in code. You create a new `dijit.layout.StackContainer` container and content panes to place in it. To place HTML in a content pane, we'll use the content pane's `domNode` property and place HTML in the content pane like this:

`page1.domNode.innerHTML="<b>Ralph Kramden</b><br>CEO";`

The example stackcontainerprogram.html mimics the previous task, but creates its container in code.

To create a stack container in code:

1. Open your Web page in a text editor.

2. Add `dojo.require("dijit.layout.ContentPane");` and `dojo.require("dijit.form.StackContainer");` statements to your code.

3. Create a new stack container and four content panes in code; then use the `page1.domNode.innerHTML` property to place HTML in each content pane. Add the content panes to the container with the `addChild` method and add two navigation buttons.

   Script 4.6 shows what your page should look like after you make the additions.

Script 4.6 Creating a stack container in code.

```
1   <html>
2     <hea-d>
3      <title>Creating Stack Containers in
4       Code</title>
(5–19)   . . .
20     <script type="text/javascript">
21       dojo.require(
22       dojo.require("dojo.parser");
23        "dijit.layout.ContentPane");
24       dojo.require(
25        "dijit.layout.StackContainer");
26       dojo.addOnLoad(function(){
27         var container = new
28       dijit.layout.StackContainer({},
29        "stack");
30       var page1 = new
31        dijit.layout.ContentPane({});
32       page1.domNode.innerHTML="<b>Ralph
33        Kramden</b><br>CEO";
34
35       var page2 = new
36        dijit.layout.ContentPane({});
37       page2.domNode.innerHTML="<b>Ed
38        Norton</b><br>VP Operations";
39
40       var page3 = new
41        dijit.layout.ContentPane({});
42       page3.domNode.innerHTML="<b>Alice
43        Kramden</b><br>VP Marketing";
44
45       var page4 = new
46        dijit.layout.ContentPane({});
47       page4.domNode.innerHTML="<b>Trixie
48        Norton</b><br>Treasurer";
49
50       container.addChild(page1);
51       container.addChild(page2);
52       container.addChild(page3);
53       container.addChild(page4);
54
55       container.startup();
56     });
57     </script>
58   </head>
59   <body class="tundra">
```

(script continues)

Script 4.6 *continued*

```
60      <h1>Creating Stack Containers in
61        Code</h1>
62      <br>
63      <div id="stack"
64        style="width:150px; height:75px;
65        border:solid 1px;">
66      </div>
67      <button
68        dojoType="dijit.form.Button">&lt;
69        <script type="dojo/method"
70          event="onClick" args="evt">
71          dijit.byId("stack").back();
72        </script>
73      </button>
74      <button
75        dojoType="dijit.form.Button">&gt;
76        <script type="dojo/method"
77          event="onClick" args="evt">
78          dijit.byId("stack").forward();
79        </script>
80      </button>
81    </body>
82  </html>
```

4. Save your file.

5. Navigate to your file in a browser. You will see a new stack container (**Figure 4.7**).

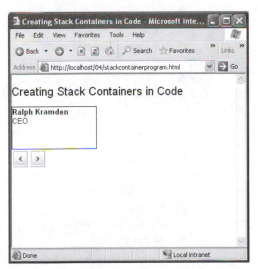

Figure 4.7 A Dijit stack container created in code.

Using TabContainer

The TabContainer container lets you place your content panes on tabbed pages. All you need to do is place content panes (with the `title` attribute set to the tab's label) inside this container. To let the user close a tab, set the content pane's `closable` attribute to "true".

The example tabcontainer.html displays four tabs, and the fourth tab can be closed (when you click the close icon, the tab disappears).

To add tab containers:

1. Open your Web page in a text editor.

2. Add `dojo.require("dijit.layout.ContentPane");` and `dojo.require("dijit.form.TabContainer");` statements to your code.

3. Create a new tab container, enclosing four content panes in it. Make the fourth tab closable, and add code to display an alert box when the content pane's `onClose` event occurs.

   Script 4.7 shows what your page should look like after you make the additions.

Script 4.7 Adding tab containers.

```
1    <html>
2      <head>
3        <title>Using
4        TabContainer</title>
5        <link rel="stylesheet"
6          type="text/css"
7          href="http://o.aolcdn.com/
8          dojo/1.1/dojo/
9          resources/dojo.css" />
10       <link rel="stylesheet"
11         type="text/css"
12         href="http://o.aolcdn.com/dojo/
13         1.1/dijit/
14         themes/tundra/tundra.css" />
15       <script
16         djConfig="parseOnLoad:true"
17         type="text/javascript"
18         src="http://o.aolcdn.com/dojo/1.1/
19           dojo/dojo.xd.js">
20       </script>
21       <script type="text/javascript">
22         dojo.require("dojo.parser");
23         dojo.require(
24           "dijit.layout.ContentPane");
25         dojo.require(
26           "dijit.layout.TabContainer");
27       </script>
28     </head>
29     <body class="tundra">
30       <h1>Using Tab Containers</h1>
31       <br>
32       <div dojoType=
33         "dijit.layout.TabContainer"
34         style="width:280px; height:100px;
35         margin:5px; border:solid 1px;">
36         <div dojoType=
37           "dijit.layout.ContentPane"
38           title="Tab 1">
39           <b>Ralph Kramden</b><br>CEO
40         </div>
41
```

(script continues)

Script **4.7** *continued*

```
42        <div dojoType=
43          "dijit.layout.ContentPane"
44          title="Tab 2">
45          <b>Ed Norton</b><br>VP Operations
46        </div>
47        <div dojoType=
48          "dijit.layout.ContentPane"
49          title="Tab 3">
50          <b>Alice Kramden</b><br>VP
51          Marketing
52        </div>
53        <div dojoType=
54          "dijit.layout.ContentPane"
55          title="Tab 4"
56          closable="true">
57          <b>Trixie Norton</b><br>Treasurer
58          <script type="dojo/method"
59            event="onClose" args="evt">
60            alert("Closing tab 4");
61            return true;
62          </script>
63        </div>
64      </div>
65    </body>
66  </html>
```

4. Save your file.

5. Navigate to your file in a browser. You should see a tab container (**Figure 4.8**).

6. Click a new tab to opening the corresponding page (**Figure 4.9**).

Script **4.8** *continued*

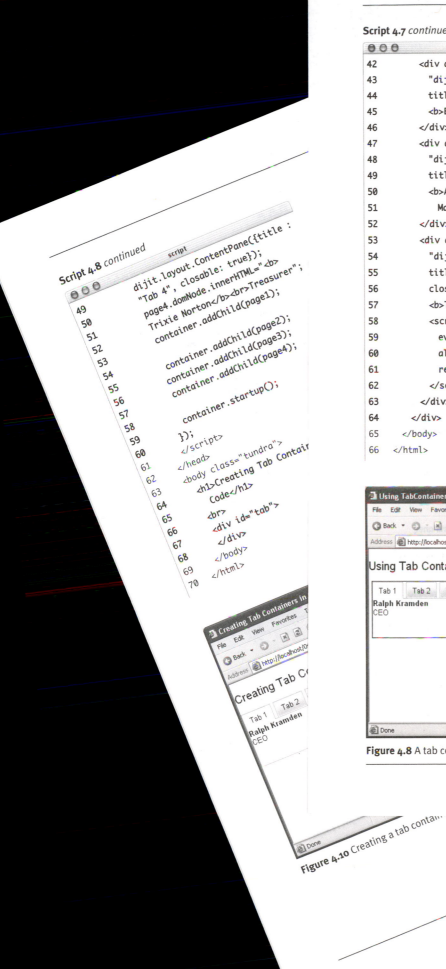

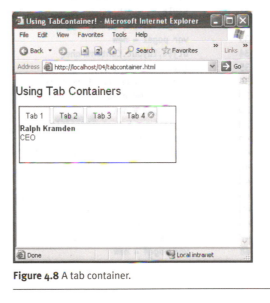

Figure 4.8 A tab container.

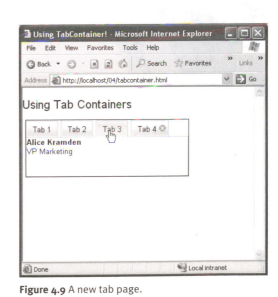

Figure 4.9 A new tab page.

Figure 4.10 Creating a tab contai...

Creating a TabContainer Dijit in Code

You can also create TabContainer layout Dijits in code. The next example, tabcontainerprogram.html, mimics the previous task. In the code, you configure the content panes by passing attributes to the ContentPane constructor, such as {title : "Tab 4", closable: true}, to set the titl and closable attributes.

To create tab containers in code:

1. Open your Web page in a text edit

2. Add dojo.require("dijit.layo ContentPane"); and dojo.requ ("dijit.form.TabContainer" statements to your code.

3. Create a new tab container content panes in it. Make closable, and add code to box when the content p event occurs.

   Script 4.8 shows wh look like after you n

APPLICATION DIJITS: TOOL TIPS AND MORE

This chapter starts our two-chapter guided tour of Dojo application Dijits. This chapter covers the Tooltip, Dialog, ProgressBar, ColorPalette, and Toolbar application Dijits.

The Tooltip Dijit adds a nice touch to any application: when the user rests the mouse cursor on over a page element, the tool tip appears.

Dialog Dijits let you pop up a dialog box that gives the user information or accepts user input.

ProgressBar Dijits are great when you have an operation that takes some time, such as a download, and you want to keep the user updated. The user can track the progress of the operation with a bar that fills up with color.

Color palettes let the user select a color from a display of multiple colors. You'll see how to use ColorPalette Dijits in both a Web page and a dialog box.

The Dojo Toolbar application Dijit lets you group buttons and other Dijits into toolbars that can be positioned anywhere you want them in the page.

There's a lot coming up in this chapter, so let's get started.

Using Tooltip

Tool tips can add a lot to applications, and users have come to expect them. They're those little windows that pop up when the mouse moves slowly over a page element. Creating a basic tool tip is easy: just give a `<div>` element the `dojoType` attribute set to `dijit.Tooltip` and set its `connectId` attribute to the ID of the element to which you want to connect the tool tip.

The example here, tooltip.html, attaches a tool tip to an accordion container.

To create a tool tip:

1. Open your Web page in a text editor.

2. Add a `dojo.require("dijit.Tooltip");` statement to your code.

3. Connect the tool tip to the element for which you want it to appear by setting its `connectId` attribute to the ID of the target element.

   Script 5.1 shows what your page should look like after you make the additions.

Script 5.1 Creating a tool tip.

```
1    <html>
2      <head>
3        <title>Using Tool Tips</title>
4
5        <link rel="stylesheet"
6          type="text/css"
7          href="http://o.aolcdn.com/
8          dojo/1.1/dojo/
9          resources/dojo.css" />
10
11       <link rel="stylesheet"
12         type="text/css"
13         href="http://o.aolcdn.com/dojo/
14         1.1/dijit/
15         themes/tundra/tundra.css" />
16
17       <script
18         djConfig="parseOnLoad:true"
19         type="text/javascript"
20         src="http://o.aolcdn.com/dojo/1.1/
21         dojo/dojo.xd.js">
22       </script>
23
24       <script type="text/javascript">
25         dojo.require("dojo.parser");
26         dojo.require(
27         "dijit.layout.ContentPane");
28         dojo.require(
29         "dijit.layout
30         .AccordionContainer");
31         dojo.require(
32         "dijit.Tooltip");
33       </script>
34     </head>
35     <body class="tundra">
36       <h1>Using Tool Tips</h1>
37       <br>
38       <div dojoType=
39         "dijit.layout.AccordionContainer"
40         style="width:150px; height:180px;
41         margin:5px">
42         <div dojoType=
43           "dijit.layout.AccordionPane"
44           title="CEO">
45           Ralph Kramden
```

(script continues)

Script 5.1 *continued*

```
46        </div>
47
48        <div dojoType=
49          "dijit.layout.AccordionPane"
50          title="VP Operations">
51          Ed Norton
52        </div>
53
54        <div dojoType=
55          "dijit.layout.AccordionPane"
56          title="VP Marketing">
57          Alice Kramden
58        </div>
59
60        <div id="blue" dojoType=
61          "dijit.layout.AccordionPane"
62          title="Treasurer">
63          Trixie Norton
64        </div>
65      </div>
66    </div>
67    <div dojoType="dijit.Tooltip"
68      connectId="accordion">
69      Our staff
70    </div>
71  </body>
72 </html>
```

4. Save your file.

5. Navigate to your file in a browser. You should see a tool tip with the text "Our staff" when the mouse cursor rests on the target element (**Figure 5.1**).

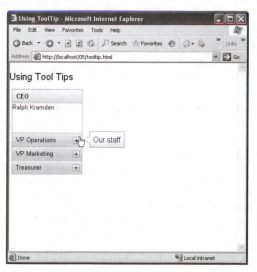

Figure 5.1 A Dijit tool tip.

Using Tooltip with Images

You can add images to tool tips simply by enclosing an `<img>` element when you create the tool tip.

The example tooltipimages.html adds an image to the tool tip you saw in the previous task: it adds an icon of a person, person.jpg, to the tool tip "Our staff."

To create a tool tip with images:

1. Open your Web page in a text editor.

2. Add a `dojo.require("dijit.Tooltip");` statement to your code.

3. Connect the tool tip to the element for which you want it to appear by setting its `connectId` attribute to the ID of the target element. Add an `<img>` element to the tool tip definition.

   Script 5.2 shows what your page should look like after you make the additions.

Script 5.2 Creating a tool tip with images.

```
1   <html>
2     <head>
3       <title>Using Tool Tips with
4         Images</title>
5       <link rel="stylesheet"
6         type="text/css"
7         href="http://o.aolcdn.com/
8         dojo/1.1/dojo/
9         resources/dojo.css" />
10      <link rel="stylesheet"
11        type="text/css"
12        href="http://o.aolcdn.com/dojo/
13        1.1/dijit/
14        themes/tundra/tundra.css" />
15      <script
16        djConfig="parseOnLoad:true"
17        type="text/javascript"
18        src="http://o.aolcdn.com/dojo/1.1/
19          dojo/dojo.xd.js">
20      </script>
21      <script type="text/javascript">
22        dojo.require("dojo.parser");
23        dojo.require(
24        "dijit.layout.ContentPane");
25        dojo.require(
26        "dijit.layout
27        .AccordionContainer");
28        dojo.require(
29        "dijit.Tooltip");
30      </script>
31    </head>
32    <body class="tundra">
33      <h1>Using Tool Tips with Images</h1>
34      <br>
35      <div dojoType=
36        "dijit.layout.AccordionContainer"
37        style="width:150px; height:180px;
38        margin:5px">
39        <div dojoType=
40          "dijit.layout.AccordionPane"
41          title="CEO">
42          Ralph Kramden
```

(script continues)

Script 5.2 *continued*

```
43        </div>
44        <div dojoType=
45          "dijit.layout.AccordionPane"
46          title="VP Operations">
47          Ed Norton
48        </div>
49        <div dojoType=
50          "dijit.layout.AccordionPane"
51          title="VP Marketing">
52          Alice Kramden
53        </div>
54        <div id="blue" dojoType=
55          "dijit.layout.AccordionPane"
56          title="Treasurer">
57          Trixie Norton
58        </div>
59      </div>
60      <div dojoType="dijit.Tooltip"
61      connectId="accordion">
62        Our staff<img src='person.jpg'/>
63      </div>
64    </body>
65  </html>
```

4. Save your file.

5. Navigate to your file in a browser. You should see a tool tip with an image when the mouse cursor rests on the target element (**Figure 5.2**).

✔ Tip

■ If you want to add more images to a tool tip, just add more `<img>` elements. For instance, here you could add a photo of each staff member.

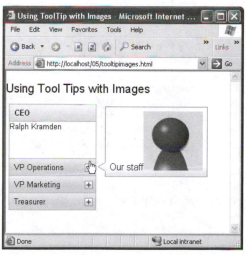

Figure 5.2 A Dijit tool tip with an image.

Using Dialog

The Dialog Dijit lets you display dialog boxes that fade in and out as they appear and disappear.

This example, dialog.html, displays a dialog box with a message "I like opera. Doesn't everybody?" when the user clicks a button. In the next task, you'll see how to accept user input in dialog boxes.

To create a dialog box:

1. Open your Web page in a text editor.

2. Add dojo.require("dijit.form.Button"); and dojo.require("dijit.Dialog"); statements to your code.

3. Create a new dialog box with the dojoType attribute set to dijit.Dialog and enclose the text you want to display in the dialog box. Have the button call the dialog box's show method to display the dialog box.

   Script 5.3 shows what your page should look like after you make the additions.

Script 5.3 Creating a dialog box.

```
1    <html>
2     <head>
3       <title>Using Dialog</title>
4
5       <link rel="stylesheet"
6        type="text/css"
7        href="http://o.aolcdn.com/
8        dojo/1.1/dojo/
9        resources/dojo.css" />
10
11      <link rel="stylesheet"
12       type="text/css"
13       href="http://o.aolcdn.com/dojo/
14       1.1/dijit/
15       themes/tundra/tundra.css" />
16
17      <script
18       djConfig="parseOnLoad:true"
19       type="text/javascript"
20       src="http://o.aolcdn.com/dojo/1.1/
21        dojo/dojo.xd.js">
22      </script>
23
24      <script type="text/javascript">
25       dojo.require("dojo.parser");
26       dojo.require("dijit.Dialog");
27       dojo.require(
28        "dijit.form.Button");
29      </script>
30     </head>
31
32     <body class="tundra">
33      <h1>Using Dialog</h1>
34      <br>
35      <button id="button" dojoType=
36       "dijit.form.Button">Click me
37       <script type="dojo/method"
38        event="onClick" args="evt">
39        dijit.byId("dialog").show();
40       </script>
41      </button>
42
43      <div id="dialog"
44       dojoType="dijit.Dialog">
45       I like opera. Doesn't everybody?
46      </div>
47     </body>
48    </html>
```

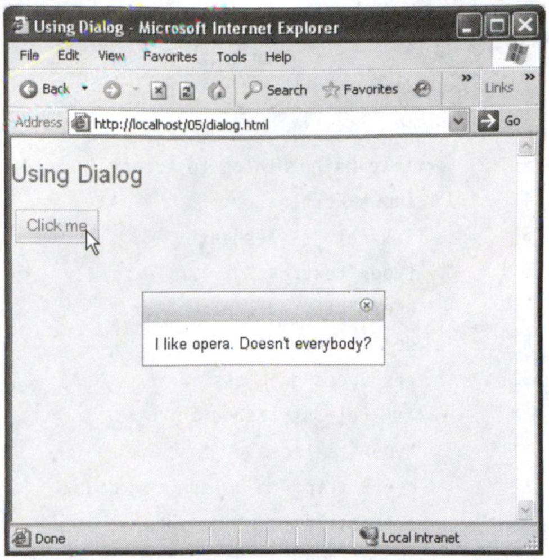

Figure 5.3 A dialog box.

4. Save your file.

5. Navigate to your file in a browser and click the button. The dialog box should appear (**Figure 5.3**).

6. Click the close button on the dialog box to dismiss it.

✔ **Tip**

■ Do you want to close a dialog box in code? Call its `hide` method, as shown in the next task.

Using Dialog with Input

Dialog boxes can also display other Dijits, such as text boxes and buttons, to let the user make entries.

The example dialoginput.html displays a dialog box with a text box and an OK button. When you enter text in the text box and click OK, the dialog box disappears and the text appears in a text box in the main Web page.

To accept input in a dialog box:

1. Open your Web page in a text editor.

2. Add dojo.require("dijit.form.Button");, dojo.require("dijit.form.TextBox");, and dojo.require("dijit.Dialog"); statements to your code.

3. Create a new dialog box with the dojoType attribute set to dijit.Dialog and enclose a text box, an OK button, and a prompt (in this case, "Enter your opinion of opera"). Connect the OK button to code that hides the dialog box and displays the entered text in a text box in the main Web page.

   Script 5.4 shows what your page should look like after you make the additions.

Script 5.4 Accepting input in a dialog box.

```
1   <html>
2     <head>
3       <title>Using Dialog to Accept
4         Input</title>
5       <link rel="stylesheet"
6         type="text/css"
7         href="http://o.aolcdn.com/
8         dojo/1.1/dojo/
9         resources/dojo.css" />
10      <link rel="stylesheet"
11        type="text/css"
12        href="http://o.aolcdn.com/dojo/
13        1.1/dijit/
14        themes/tundra/tundra.css" />
15      <script
16        djConfig="parseOnLoad:true"
17        type="text/javascript"
18        src="http://o.aolcdn.com/dojo/1.1/
19          dojo/dojo.xd.js">
20      </script>
21
22      <script type="text/javascript">
23        dojo.require("dojo.parser");
24        dojo.require("dijit.Dialog");
25        dojo.require(
26          "dijit.form.Button");
27        dojo.require("dijit.form.TextBox");
28      </script>
29    </head>
30
31    <body class="tundra">
32      <h1>Using Dialog to Accept
33        Input</h1>
34      <br>
35      <button id="button" dojoType=
36        "dijit.form.Button">Click me
37        <script type="dojo/method"
38          event="onClick" args="evt">
39          dijit.byId("dialog").show();
40        </script>
41      </button>
42
```

(script continues)

Script 5.4 *continued*

```
43      <div id="dialog" dojoType=
44         "dijit.Dialog">
45         Enter your opinion of opera.
46         <input id="text" dojoType=
47            "dijit.form.TextBox"></input>
48         <button id="OKbutton" dojoType=
49            "dijit.form.Button">OK
50          <script type="dojo/method"
51            event="onClick" args="evt">
52            dijit.byId("dialog").hide();
53            dijit.byId("result")
54              .setValue("You entered: " +
55              dijit.byId("text").getValue());
56          </script>
57         </button>
58      </div>
59      <input id="result" dojoType=
60         "dijit.form.TextBox"></input>
61    </body>
62  </html>
```

4. Save your file.

5. Navigate to your file in a browser and click the button. You should see a dialog box (**Figure 5.4**).

6. Enter text in the text box and click the OK button. The text you entered should appear in the text box in the main Web page (**Figure 5.5**).

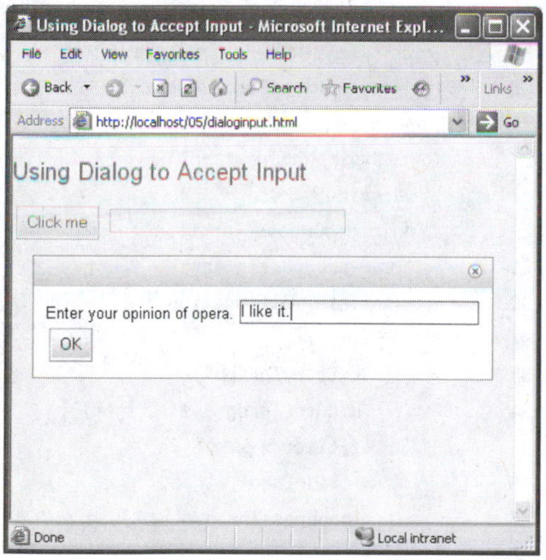

Figure 5.4 A dialog box that accepts input.

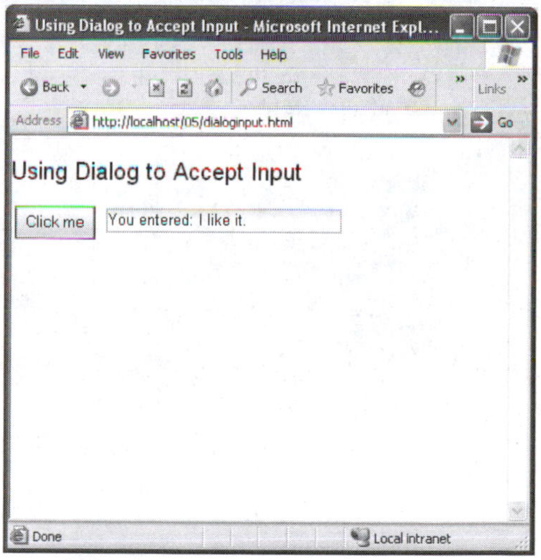

Figure 5.5 Reading text input in a dialog box.

Using ProgressBar

You use progress bars to keep the user apprised of some time-consuming operation, such as downloading of data. A progress bar fills with color as the operation progresses from 0% to 100% complete.

The example progressbar.html uses a Java-Script timer to make a progress bar move from 0% to 100% in a few seconds. The code uses the progress bar's update method to update its progress attribute like this, where timer is the value of the timer: dijit.byId ("pb").update({progress : timer});

To create a progress bar:

1. Open your Web page in a text editor.

2. Add a dojo.require("dijit. ProgressBar"); statement to your code.

3. Create a new progress bar with dojoType set to dijit.ProgressBar. Set up a JavaScript timer to update the progress bar's progress attribute every 50 milliseconds with a steadily increasing value.

   Script 5.5 shows what your page should look like after you make the additions.

Script 5.5 Creating a progress bar.

```
1    <html>
2      <head>
3        <title>Using Progress Bars</title>
4
5        <link rel="stylesheet"
6          type="text/css"
7          href="http://o.aolcdn.com/
8          dojo/1.1/dojo/
9          resources/dojo.css" />
10
11       <link rel="stylesheet"
12         type="text/css"
13         href="http://o.aolcdn.com/dojo/
14         1.1/dijit/
15         themes/tundra/tundra.css" />
16
17       <script
18         djConfig="parseOnLoad:true"
19         type="text/javascript"
20         src="http://o.aolcdn.com/dojo/1.1/
21           dojo/dojo.xd.js">
22       </script>
23
24       <script type="text/javascript">
25         dojo.require("dojo.parser");
26         dojo.require(
27           "dijit.ProgressBar");
28         var timer = 0;
29         dojo.addOnLoad(function() {
30           var progressInterval =
31           setInterval(function() {
32             timer++;
33             dijit.byId("pb")
34             .update({progress : timer});
35             if(timer > 100){
36               clearInterval(
37               progressInterval);
38             }
39           }, 50);
40         });
41       </script>
42     </head>
```

(script continues)

Script 5.5 *continued*

```
44      <body class="tundra">
45        <h1>Using Progress Bars</h1>
46        <br>
47        <div id="pb"
48          dojoType="dijit.ProgressBar"
49          style="width:200px"></div>
50        </div>
51      </body>
52    </html>
```

Figure 5.6 A progress bar.

4. Save your file.

5. Navigate to your file in a browser. You should see a progress bar that fills in a few seconds (**Figure 5.6**).

Using ColorPalette

The ColorPalette Dijit lets users select a color from a palette control—a great aid when you want users to be able to customize pages with a background color, personalize email, or select a drawing color. This control displays a table of colors that the user can click.

In the example colorpalette.html, when the user clicks a color in the palette, its onChange event occurs, and the event handling function is passed the new color as a hexadecimal string (the same format as you use for colors in Web pages).

To create a color palette:

1. Open your Web page in a text editor.

2. Add a dojo.require("dijit.ColorPalette"); statement to your code.

3. Create a new color palette and connect its onChange event to a script that displays the newly selected color in an alert box.

   Script 5.6 shows what your page should look like after you make the additions.

Script 5.6 Creating a color palette.

```
1    <html>
2      <head>
3        <title>Using Color Palettes</title>
4
5        <link rel="stylesheet"
6          type="text/css"
7          href="http://o.aolcdn.com/
8          dojo/1.1/dojo/
9          resources/dojo.css" />
10
11       <link rel="stylesheet"
12         type="text/css"
13         href="http://o.aolcdn.com/dojo/
14         1.1/dijit/
15         themes/tundra/tundra.css" />
16
17       <script
18         djConfig="parseOnLoad:true"
19         type="text/javascript"
20         src="http://o.aolcdn.com/dojo/1.1/
21           dojo/dojo.xd.js">
22       </script>
23
24       <script type="text/javascript">
25         dojo.require("dojo.parser");
26         dojo.require(
27           "dijit.ColorPalette");
28       </script>
29     </head>
30
31     <body class="tundra">
32       <h1>Using Color Palettes</h1>
33       <br>
34       <div dojoType="dijit.ColorPalette">
35         <script type="dojo/method"
36         event="onChange"
37         args="selectedColor">
38         alert("You selected : " +
39         selectedColor);
40         </script>
41       </div>
42     </body>
43   </html>
```

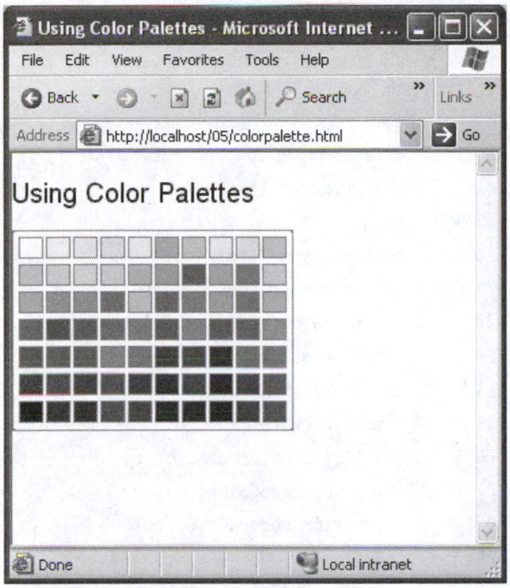

Figure 5.7 A Dijit color palette.

Figure 5.8 Selecting a color.

4. Save your file.

5. Navigate to your file in a browser. You should see the color palette (**Figure 5.7**).

6. Double-click a color in the palette. The hexadecimal value of the color you selected appears in an alert box (**Figure 5.8**).

✔ Tip

- The next task discusses how to display a color palette in a dialog box.

Using ColorPalette with Dialog

You can let the user select colors from a color palette in a dialog box. Such a dialog box is often called a *color picker* or *color chooser*.

The next example, colorpalettedialog.html, lets the user select a color in a dialog box and then stores that color value internally. When the user closes the dialog box, the selected color is displayed in an alert box.

To create a color picker dialog box:

1. Open your Web page in a text editor.

2. Add dojo.require("dijit.Dialog");, dojo.require("dijit.form.Button");, and dojo.require("dijit.Color Palette"); statements to your code.

3. Create a new dialog box with a color palette and an OK button and connect its onChange event to a function that stores the color that the user selected. When the user clicks the OK button to close the dialog box, display the selected color in an alert box.

   Script 5.7 shows what your page should look like after you make the additions.

Script 5.7 Creating a color picker dialog box.

```
1    <html>
2      <head>
3       <title>Using ColorPalette in a
4        Dialog</title>
(5–19) . . .
20      <script type="text/javascript">
21        dojo.require("dojo.parser");
22        dojo.require("dijit.Dialog");
23        dojo.require(
24          "dijit.form.Button");
25        dojo.require(
26          "dijit.ColorPalette");
27        var selectedColor;
28        function recordColor(color)
29        {
30          selectedColor = color;
31        }
32        function displayColor()
33        {
34          alert("You chose " +
35          selectedColor);
36        }
37       </script>
38      </head>
39     <body class="tundra">
40       <h1>Using ColorPalette in a
41        Dialog</h1>
42       <br>
43       <button id="button" dojoType=
44       "dijit.form.Button">Click me
45         <script type="dojo/method"
46           event="onClick" args="evt">
47           dijit.byId("dialog").show();
48         </script>
49       </button>
50       <div id="dialog" dojoType=
51        "dijit.Dialog">
52         Pick your color...
53         <div id="cp" dojoType=
54         "dijit.ColorPalette">
55          <script type="dojo/method" event=
```

(script continues)

Script 5.7 *continued*

```
56          "onChange" args="selectedColor">
57          recordColor(selectedColor);
58        </script>
59      </div>
60      <button id="OKbutton" dojoType=
61        "dijit.form.Button">OK
62        <script type="dojo/method" event=
63          "onClick" args="evt">
64          dijit.byId("dialog").hide();
65          displayColor();
66        </script>
67      </button>
68    </div>
69  </body>
70  </html>
```

4. Save your file.

5. Navigate to your file in a browser and click the Click me button. You should see the dialog box with the color palette (**Figure 5.9**).

6. Click a color and click the OK button. You should see the color you selected displayed in an alert box (**Figure 5.10**).

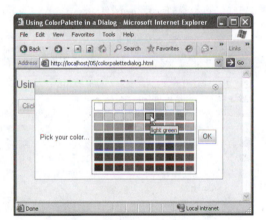

Figure 5.9 A color picker dialog box.

Figure 5.10 The color you selected.

Using Toolbar

The Toolbar Dijit let you arrange buttons in—you guessed it—a toolbar. It's super easy to use: just enclose buttons inside a Toolbar Dijit.

The example toolbar.html arranges four buttons in a toolbar, each of which displays an alert box when clicked. To create this example, you enclose four buttons in a toolbar and connect each of them to an alert box.

To create a toolbar:

1. Open your Web page in a text editor.

2. Add dojo.require("dijit.Toolbar"); and dojo.require("dijit.form. Button"); statements to your code.

3. Create a new toolbar with four buttons and connect each button to an alert box.
   Script 5.8 shows what your page should look like after you make the additions.

Script 5.8 Creating a toolbar.

```
1   <html>
2     <head>
3       <title>Using Toolbar</title>
4
5       <link rel="stylesheet"
6         type="text/css"
7         href="http://o.aolcdn.com/
8         dojo/1.1/dojo/
9         resources/dojo.css" />
10
11      <link rel="stylesheet"
12        type="text/css"
13        href="http://o.aolcdn.com/dojo/
14        1.1/dijit/
15        themes/tundra/tundra.css" />
16
17      <script
18        djConfig="parseOnLoad:true"
19        type="text/javascript"
20        src="http://o.aolcdn.com/dojo/1.1/
21        dojo/dojo.xd.js">
22      </script>
23
24      <script type="text/javascript">
25        dojo.require("dojo.parser");
26        dojo.require(
27          "dijit.Toolbar");
28        dojo.require(
29          "dijit.form.Button");
30      </script>
31    </head>
32
33    <body class="tundra">
34      <h1>Using Toolbar<h1>
35      <div dojoType="dijit.Toolbar"
36        style="width:300px">
37        <button id="button1" dojoType=
38          "dijit.form.Button">Click me
39          <script type="dojo/method"
40            event="onClick" args="evt">
41            alert("You clicked button 1.");
42          </script>
43        </button>
44        <button id="button2" dojoType=
45          "dijit.form.Button">Click me
```

(script continues)

Script 5.8 *continued*

```
46          <script type="dojo/method"
47            event="onClick" args="evt">
48            alert("You clicked button 2.");
49          </script>
50        </button>
51        <button id="button3" dojoType=
52          "dijit.form.Button">Click me
53          <script type="dojo/method"
54            event="onClick" args="evt">
55            alert("You clicked button 3.");
56          </script>
57        </button>
58        <button id="button4" dojoType=
59          "dijit.form.Button">Click me
60          <script type="dojo/method"
61            event="onClick" args="evt">
62            alert("You clicked button 4.");
63          </script>
64        </button>
65      </div>
66    </body>
67  </html>
```

4. Save your file.

5. Navigate to your file in a browser. You should see the buttons arranged in a toolbar (**Figure 5.11**).

6. Click a button. You should see an alert box confirming the button click (**Figure 5.12**).

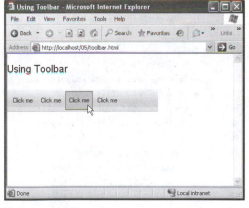

Figure 5.11 A Dijit toolbar.

Figure 5.12 A Dijit toolbar.

Adding Images to Toolbar Buttons

You can add images to toolbar buttons: for example, icons for operations such as editing, copying, and so on that the buttons on your toolbar support.

This example, toolbarimage.html, displays the person icon (person.jpg) from the tool tip example earlier in this chapter in a toolbar's buttons.

To create a toolbar with images:

1. Open your Web page in a text editor.

2. Add `dojo.require("dijit.Toolbar");` and `dojo.require("dijit.form. Button");` statements to your code.

3. Create a new toolbar with four buttons and connect each button to an alert box. Add an image to each button by nesting `<img src="person.jpg">` elements in each button.

   Script 5.9 shows what your page should look like after you make the additions.

Script 5.9 Creating a toolbar with images.

```
1    <html>
2      <head>
3        <title>Using Toolbar and
4        Images</title>
5        <link rel="stylesheet"
6        type="text/css"
7        href="http://o.aolcdn.com/
8        dojo/1.1/dojo/
9        resources/dojo.css" />
10       <link rel="stylesheet"
11       type="text/css"
12       href="http://o.aolcdn.com/dojo/
13       1.1/dijit/
14       themes/tundra/tundra.css" />
15       <script
16       djConfig="parseOnLoad:true"
17       type="text/javascript"
18       src="http://o.aolcdn.com/dojo/1.1/
19         dojo/dojo.xd.js">
20       </script>
21       <script type="text/javascript">
22         dojo.require("dojo.parser");
23         dojo.require(
24           "dijit.Toolbar");
25         dojo.require(
26           "dijit.form.Button");
27       </script>
28     </head>
29     <body class="tundra">
30       <h1>Using Toolbar and Images</h1>
31       <div dojoType="dijit.Toolbar"
32         style="width:700px">
33         <button id="button1" dojoType=
34           "dijit.form.Button">Click me
35           <img src="person.jpg">
36           <script type="dojo/method"
37           event="onClick" args="evt">
38           alert("You clicked button 1");
39           </script>
40         </button>
41         <button id="button1" dojoType=
42           "dijit.form.Button">Click me
43           <img src="person.jpg">
44           <script type="dojo/method"
45           event="onClick" args="evt">
```

(script continues)

Script 5.9 *continued*

```
46              alert("You clicked button 1");
47          </script>
48      </button>
49      <button id="button1" dojoType=
50          "dijit.form.Button">Click me
51          <img src="person.jpg">
52          <script type="dojo/method"
53          event="onClick" args="evt">
54          alert("You clicked button 1");
55          </script>
56      </button>
57      <button id="button1" dojoType=
58          "dijit.form.Button">Click me
59          <img src="person.jpg">
60          <script type="dojo/method"
61          event="onClick" args="evt">
62          alert("You clicked button 1");
63          </script>
64      </button>
65      </div>
66  </body>
67 </html>
```

4. Save your file.

5. Navigate to your file in a browser. You should see the toolbar with the images (**Figure 5.13**).

6. Click a button in the toolbar. You should see an alert box indicating the button you clicked (**Figure 5.14**).

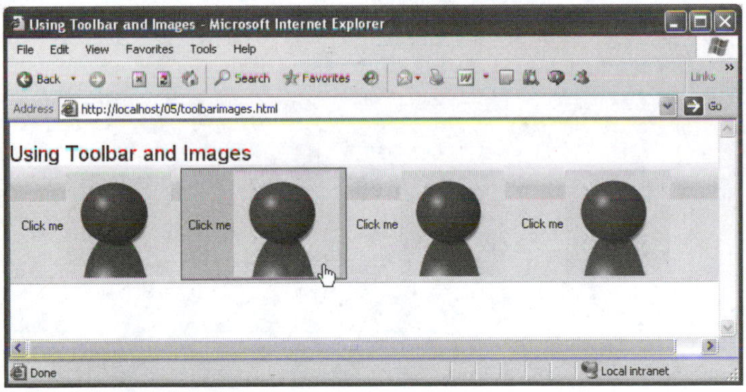

Figure 5.13 A toolbar with images.

Figure 5.14 Clicking a toolbar button.

APPLICATION DIJITS: MENUS, TREES, AND MORE

6

This chapter offers more popular Dijits: menus, title panes, inline edit boxes, and trees.

Menus in Dojo are presented much like open `<select>` controls—and you need to do a little work to get them to drop down in the way familiar to menu users everywhere. You'll also see how to create context menus that you can make appear with a right-click of the mouse.

Title panes give their content a title, and their content is collapsible, and therefore can be hidden.

Inline edit boxes can be used to edit the text in a page. Using these Dijits, you can edit a page, such as a form letter, and then print the page on a printer.

Trees list data items in tree format, with collapsible nodes. Trees are a familiar control to anyone who uses Windows Explorer, for example, and you see how to add your own nodes to a tree structure here.

We have a lot to cover, so let's get started.

Using Menu

Standard menus in Dojo may not be what you expect: they look like open `<select>` controls, presenting a list of clickable items, and such a menu is always open. You'll see how to create traditional menus that open and close later in the chapter.

The example here, menu.html, creates a menu containing three items—Tic, Tac, and Toe—and when the user clicks an item, the code displays an alert box containing the item's name (Tic, Tac, or Toe).

To create a menu:

1. Open your Web page in a text editor.

2. Add a `dojo.require("dijit.Menu");` statement to your code.

3. Create a new `<div>` element with `dojoType` set to `dijit.Menu` and three `<div>` elements inside it, with `dojoType` set to `dijit.MenuItem`. Add a click event handler to each menu item.

   Script 6.1 shows what your page should look like after you make the additions.

Script 6.1 Creating a menu.

```
1   <html>
2     <head>
3       <title>Using Menus</title>
4       <link rel="stylesheet"
5         type="text/css"
6         href="http://o.aolcdn.com/
7         dojo/1.1/dojo/
8         resources/dojo.css" />
9       <link rel="stylesheet"
10        type="text/css"
11        href="http://o.aolcdn.com/dojo/
12        1.1/dijit/
13        themes/tundra/tundra.css" />
14      <script
15        djConfig="parseOnLoad:true"
16        type="text/javascript"
17        src="http://o.aolcdn.com/dojo/1.1/
18        dojo/dojo.xd.js">
19      </script>
20      <script type="text/javascript">
21        dojo.require("dojo.parser");
22        dojo.require("dijit.Menu");
23      </script>
24    </head>
25    <body class="tundra">
26      <h1>Using Menus</h1>
27      <div dojoType="dijit.Menu">
28        <div dojoType="dijit.MenuItem">Tic
29          <script type="dojo/method"
30          event="onClick" args="evt">
31            alert("Tic");
32          </script>
33        </div>
34        <div dojoType="dijit.MenuItem">Tac
35          <script type="dojo/method"
36          event="onClick" args="evt">
37            alert("Tac");
38          </script>
39        </div>
40        <div dojoType="dijit.MenuItem">Toe
41          <script type="dojo/method"
42            event="onClick" args="evt">
43              alert("Toe");
44          </script>
45        </div>
46      </div>
47    </body>
48  </html>
```

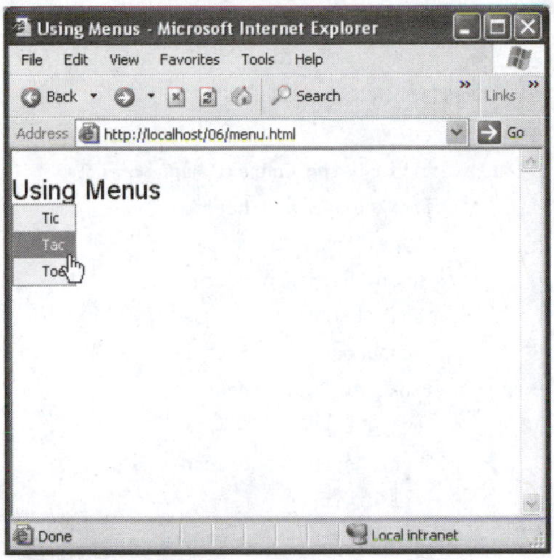

Figure 6.1 A Dijit menu.

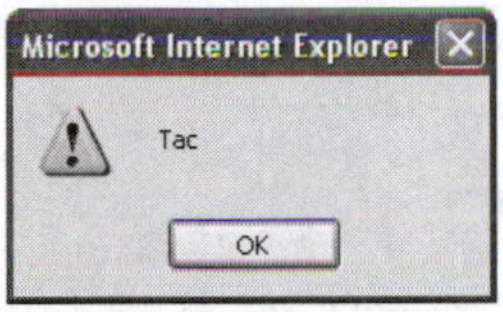

Figure 6.2 Clicking a
menu item.

4. Save your file.

5. Navigate to your file in a browser. You should see the menu (**Figure 6.1**).

6. Click a menu item. You should see an alert box displaying the menu item's name (**Figure 6.2**).

✔ **Tip**

■ This menu is styled on a context menu, coming up next, and it may not be what you picture when you think of a menu. We'll create traditional menus later in the chapter.

Creating Context Menus

Dijit menus are ideal as context menus: those menus that appear at the mouse location when you right-click an element.

The next example, contextmenu.html, displays a colored `<div>` element, which, when right-clicked, displays a context menu.

To create a context menu:

1. Open your Web page in a text editor.

2. Add a `dojo.require("dijit.Menu");` statement to your code.

3. Create a new `<div>` element with a colored background. Create a new `<div>` element with `dojoType` set to `dijit.Menu`, its `targetNodeIds` attribute set to the ID of the first `<div>` element, and three `<div>` elements inside it, with `dojoType` set to `dijit.MenuItem`. Add a click event handler to each menu item.

Script 6.2 shows what your page should look like after you make the additions.

Script 6.2 Creating a context menu.

```
1   <html>
2     <head>
3       <title>Using Context Menus</title>
4       <link rel="stylesheet"
5         type="text/css"
6         href="http://o.aolcdn.com/
7         dojo/1.1/dojo/
8         resources/dojo.css" />
9       <link rel="stylesheet"
10        type="text/css"
11        href="http://o.aolcdn.com/dojo/
12        1.1/dijit/
13        themes/tundra/tundra.css" />
14      <script
15        djConfig="parseOnLoad:true"
16        type="text/javascript"
17        src="http://o.aolcdn.com/dojo/1.1/
18          dojo/dojo.xd.js">
19      </script>
20      <script type="text/javascript">
21        dojo.require("dojo.parser");
22        dojo.require("dijit.Menu");
23      </script>
24    </head>
25    <body class="tundra">
26      <h1>Using Context Menus</h1>
27      <div id="context"
28        style="background:#ddd;
29        height:200px; width:200px;"></div>
30      <div dojoType="dijit.Menu"
31        targetNodeIds="context"
32        style="display:none">
33        <div dojoType="dijit.MenuItem">Tic
34          <script type="dojo/method"
35          event="onClick" args="evt">
36            alert("Tic");
37          </script>
38        </div>
39        <div dojoType="dijit.MenuItem">Tac
40          <script type="dojo/method"
41          event="onClick" args="evt">
```

(script continues)

Script 6.2 *continued*

```
42            alert("Tac");
43          </script>
44        </div>
45        <div dojoType="dijit.MenuItem">Toe
46          <script type="dojo/method"
47          event="onClick" args="evt">
48            alert("Toe");
49          </script>
50        </div>
51      </div>
52    </body>
53  </html>
```

4. Save your file.

5. Navigate to your file in a browser and right-click the `<div>` element. You should see the context menu (**Figure 6.3**).

As in the previous task, selecting an item in the context menu displays an alert box with that item's name.

✔ Tip

■ Do you want to add a context menu to the whole window? Set the menu's `contextualMenuForWindow` attribute to `"true"`.

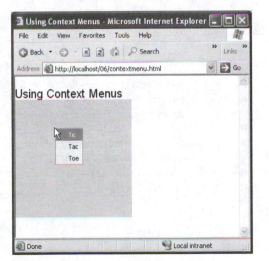

Figure 6.3 A Dijit context menu.

Creating Pop-Up Menus

You can also create submenus in Dojo, using pop-up menus that appear when you click another menu item.

The example contextmenupopup.html adds a pop-up menu containing three items—Chocolate, Vanilla, and Strawberry—to a context menu.

To create a pop-up menu:

1. Open your Web page in a text editor.

2. Add a dojo.require("dijit.Menu"); statement to your code.

3. Create a new <div> element with a colored background. Create a new <div> element with dojoType set to dijit.Menu, its targetNodeIds attribute set to the ID of the first <div> element, and three <div> elements inside it, with dojoType set to dijit.MenuItem. Set the third menu item's dojoType attribute to dijit.PopupMenuItem and add three new menu items inside the menu item. Add a click event handler to each menu item.

   Script 6.3 shows what your page should look like after you make the additions.

Script 6.3 Creating pop-up menu.

```
1    <html>
2      <head>
3        <title>Using Pop-Up Menus</title>
(4–18)  . . .
19       <script type="text/javascript">
20         dojo.require("dojo.parser");
21         dojo.require("dijit.Menu");
22       </script>
23     </head>
24     <body class="tundra">
25       <h1>Using Pop-Up Menus</h1>
26       <div id="context" style=
27         "background:#ddd; height:200px;
28         width:200px;"></div>
29       <div dojoType="dijit.Menu
30         targetNodeIds="context"
31         style="display:none">
32         <div dojoType=
33           "dijit.MenuItem">Tic
34           <script type="dojo/method"
35           event="onClick" args="evt">
36             alert("Tic");
37           </script>
38         </div>
39         <div dojoType="dijit.MenuItem">Tac
40           <script type="dojo/method"
41           event="onClick" args="evt">
42             alert("Tac");
43           </script>
44         </div>
45         <div dojoType=
46           "dijit.PopupMenuItem">
47           <span>Toe</span>
48           <div dojoType="dijit.Menu">
49             <div dojoType=
50               "dijit.MenuItem">Chocolate
51               <script type="dojo/method"
52               event="onClick" args="evt">
53               alert("Chocolate");
54             </script>
55           </div>
56           <div dojoType=
57             "dijit.MenuItem">Vanilla
58             <script type="dojo/method"
59               event="onClick" args="evt">
```

(script continues)

Script 6.3 *continued*

```
60            alert("Vanilla");
61          </script>
62        </div>
63        <div dojoType=
64          "dijit.MenuItem">Strawberry
65          <script type="dojo/method"
66            event="onClick" args="evt">
67            alert("Strawberry");
68          </script>
69        </div>
70      </div>
71    </div>
72   </div>
73  </body>
74 </html>
```

4. Save your file.

5. Navigate to your file in a browser and right-click the colored `<div>` element.

You should see the context menu appear.

6. Select the third menu item, making the pop-up menu open (**Figure 6.4**).

Selecting an item in the pop-up menu displays an alert box containing the name of the item.

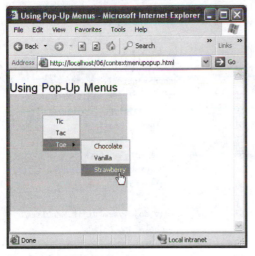

Figure 6.4 A Dijit pop-up menu.

Creating Traditional Menus

The previous tasks demonstrated that Dijit menus work well as context menus. What about creating traditional menus, with menu bars? For that, you use toolbars and drop-down buttons.

The next example, traditionalmenu.html, creates a menu bar and three drop-down menus.

To create a traditional menu:

1. Open your Web page in a text editor.

2. Add a dojo.require("dijit.Menu"); statement to your code.

3. Create a new toolbar containing three drop-down buttons and add a menu in each drop-down button; then add menu items to the three menus and click handlers for each menu item.

   Script 6.4 shows what your page should look like after you make the additions.

Script 6.4 Creating a traditional menu.

```
1    <html>
2      <head>
3        <title>Creating Traditional
         Menus</title>
(4–18)  . . .
19       <script type="text/javascript">
20         dojo.require("dojo.parser");
21         dojo.require("dijit.Toolbar");
22         dojo.require("dijit.Menu");
23         dojo.require("dijit.form.Button");
24       </script>
25     </head>
26   <body class="tundra">
27     <h1>Creating Traditional Menus</h1>
28       <div dojoType="dijit.Toolbar"
29       style="width:700px">
30         <button dojoType=
31         "dijit.form.DropDownButton">
(32–44) . . .
45         </button>
46         <button dojoType=
47         "dijit.form.DropDownButton">
48         <span>Vegetables</span>
49         <div dojoType="dijit.Menu">
50           <div dojoType="dijit.MenuItem"
51           label="Peas">
52           <script type="dojo/method"
53             event="onClick" args="evt">
54             alert("You clicked Peas");
55           </script>
56         </div>
57         <div dojoType="dijit.MenuItem"
58         label="Broccoli">
59         <script type="dojo/method"
60           event="onClick" args="evt">
61           alert("You clicked Broccoli");
62         </script>
63         </div>
64       </div>
65       </button>
66       <button dojoType=
67       "dijit.form.DropDownButton">
68       <span>Ice cream</span>
69       <div dojoType="dijit.Menu">
70         <div dojoType="dijit.MenuItem"
```

(script continues)

Script 6.4 *continued*

```
71              label="Strawberry">
72              <script type="dojo/method"
73                event="onClick" args="evt">
74                alert("You clicked
75                Strawberry");
76              </script>
77            </div>
78            <div dojoType="dijit.MenuItem"
79              label="Chocolate">
80              <script type="dojo/method"
81                event="onClick" args="evt">
82                alert("You clicked
83                Chocolate");
84              </script>
85            </div>
86            <div dojoType="dijit.MenuItem"
87              label="Vanilla">
88              <script type="dojo/method"
89                event="onClick" args="evt">
90                alert("You clicked Vanilla");
91              </script>
92            </div>
93          </div>
94        </button>
95      </div>
96    </body>
97  </html>
```

4. Save your file.

5. Navigate to your file in a browser. You should see a menu bar, which opens to display menu items when you click a menu button (**Figure 6.5**).

Figure 6.5 A traditional menu bar.

Adding Menu Separators

You can also create menu separators with Dojo. You use such separators to separate menu items visually—the separators appear as thin black lines—and to organize your menu items into groups.

The example menuseparator.html adds two menu separators to three menu items.

To create menu separators:

1. Open your Web page in a text editor.

2. Add a dojo.require("dijit.Menu"); statement to your code.

3. Create a new menu and add three menu items to it. Then add two new <div> elements with the dojoType attribute set to dijit.MenuSeparator.

   Script 6.5 shows what your page should look like after you make the additions.

Script 6.5 Creating menu separators.

```
1   <html>
2   <html>
3     <head>
4       <title>Using Menu Separators</title>
5
6       <link rel="stylesheet"
7         type="text/css"
8         href="http://o.aolcdn.com/
9         dojo/1.1/dojo/
10        resources/dojo.css" />
11
12      <link rel="stylesheet"
13        type="text/css"
14        href="http://o.aolcdn.com/dojo/
15        1.1/dijit/
16        themes/tundra/tundra.css" />
17
18      <script
19        djConfig="parseOnLoad:true"
20        type="text/javascript"
21        src="http://o.aolcdn.com/dojo/1.1/
22          dojo/dojo.xd.js">
23      </script>
24
25      <script type="text/javascript">
26        dojo.require("dojo.parser");
27        dojo.require("dijit.Menu");
28      </script>
29    </head>
30
31    <body class="tundra">
32      <h1>Using Menu Separators</h1>
33
34      <div dojoType="dijit.Menu" >
35
36        <div dojoType="dijit.MenuItem">Tic
37          <script type="dojo/method"
38            event="onClick" args="evt">
39            alert("Tac");
40          </script>
41        </div>
42
43        <div  dojoType=
44          "dijit.MenuSeparator">
45        </div>
```

(script continues)

Script 6.5 *continued*

```
46
47        <div dojoType="dijit.MenuItem">Tac
48          <script type="dojo/method"
49            event="onClick" args="evt">
50            alert("Tac");
51          </script>
52        </div>
53
54        <div dojoType=
55          "dijit.MenuSeparator">
56        </div>
57
58        <div dojoType="dijit.MenuItem">Toe
59          <script type="dojo/method"
60            event="onClick" args="evt">
61            alert("Toe");
62          </script>
63        </div>
64
65      </div>
66    </body>
67  </html>
```

4. Save your file.

5. Navigate to your file in a browser. You should see the new menu with two menu separators (**Figure 6.6**).

Figure 6.6 Using menu separators.

Using TitlePane

Title panes are slick Dijits that display items in a titled box. The items can be hidden, when the user clicks the down arrow in the title bar. This Dijit is particularly useful for displaying lists of items, such as names of contacts or a set of links.

This example, titlepane.html, displays four flavors of ice cream. When you click the arrow in the title bar, the list box closes.

To create a title pane:

1. Open your Web page in a text editor.

2. Add a dojo.require("dijit.Title Pane"); statement to your code.

3. Create a new <div> element and set the <div> element's dojoType attribute to dijit.TitlePane. Enclose a list of items using an HTML unordered list (that is, use a <ul> list).

   Script 6.6 shows what your page should look like after you make the additions.

Script 6.6 Creating a title pane.

```
1   <html>
2     <head>
3       <title>Using Title Panes</title>
4
5       <link rel="stylesheet"
6         type="text/css"
7         href="http://o.aolcdn.com/
8         dojo/1.1/dojo/
9         resources/dojo.css" />
10
11      <link rel="stylesheet"
12        type="text/css"
13        href="http://o.aolcdn.com/dojo/
14        1.1/dijit/
15        themes/tundra/tundra.css" />
16
17      <script
18        djConfig="parseOnLoad:true"
19        type="text/javascript"
20        src="http://o.aolcdn.com/dojo/1.1/
21          dojo/dojo.xd.js">
22      </script>
23
24      <script type="text/javascript">
25        dojo.require("dojo.parser");
26        dojo.require("dijit.TitlePane");
27      </script>
28    </head>
29
30    <body class="tundra">
31      <h1>Using Title Panes</h1>
32      <div dojoType="dijit.TitlePane"
33        title="Ice Cream"
34        style="width:300px">
35        <ul>
36          <li>Strawberry</li>
37          <li>Vanilla</li>
38          <li>Chocolate</li>
39          <li>Pistachio</li>
40        </ul>
41      </div>
42    </body>
43  </html>
```

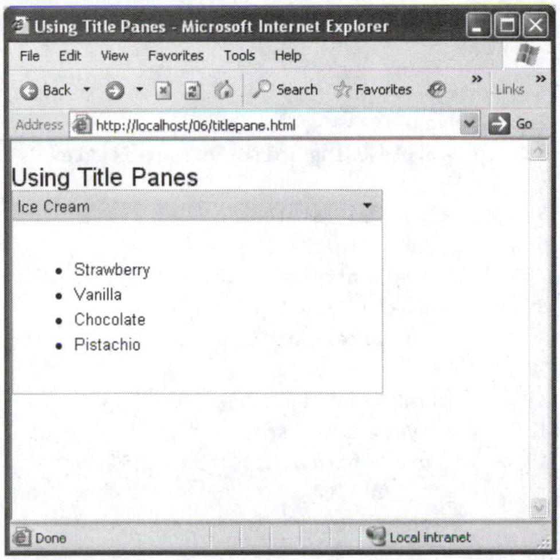

Figure 6.7 A Dijit title pane.

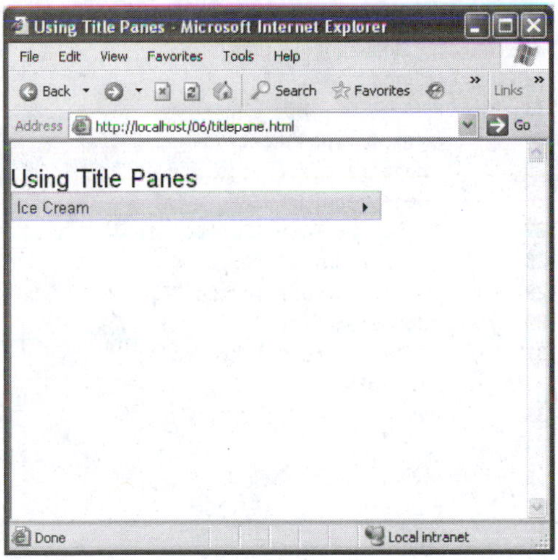

Figure 6.8 A closed Dijit title pane.

4. Save your file.

5. Navigate to your file in a browser. You should see the title pane showing the unordered list (**Figure 6.7**).

6. Click the arrow in the title bar. The title pane closes (**Figure 6.8**).

✔ Tip

■ Use an ordered list (HTML <ol>) to create a list of numbered steps as part of a quick help user guide for common tasks. You can call the title pane's `toggle` method to close or open the pane (for example, to close it for the first time it's displayed).

Using InlineEditBox

You use InlineEditBox to let the user edit text in your Web page. That's a cool thing—being able to edit the text in a Web page. These edit boxes use existing Dijits such as text boxes and text areas and allow their text to be edited it when the text is clicked. You set the type of Dijit used for the editor with the editor attribute.

This example, inlineeditbox.html, displays a form letter with InlineEditBox Dijits for the greeting, body, and signature; after editing, the form letter can be printed. You can display HTML in an inline edit box by setting the renderAsHtml attribute to "true".

To create an inline edit box:

1. Open your Web page in a text editor.

2. Add dojo.require("dijit.InlineEdit Box");, dojo.require("dijit.form. TextBox");, and dojo.require("dijit. form.Textarea"); statements to your code.

3. Create an editable form letter with a new inline edit box for the greeting (using a TextBox Dijit), body (using a Textarea Dijit), and signature (using another TextBox Dijit).

   Script 6.7 shows what your page should look like after you make the additions.

Script 6.7 Creating an inline edit box.

```
1   <html>
2     <head>
3       <title>Using InlineEditBox</title>
4
5       <link rel="stylesheet"
6         type="text/css"
7         href="http://o.aolcdn.com/
8         dojo/1.1/dojo/
9         resources/dojo.css" />
10
11      <link rel="stylesheet"
12        type="text/css"
13        href="http://o.aolcdn.com/dojo/
14        1.1/dijit/
15        themes/tundra/tundra.css" />
16
17      <script
18        djConfig="parseOnLoad:true"
19        type="text/javascript"
20        src="http://o.aolcdn.com/dojo/1.1/
21        dojo/dojo.xd.js">
22      </script>
23
24      <script type="text/javascript">
25        dojo.require("dojo.parser");
26        dojo.require(
27          "dijit.InlineEditBox");
28        dojo.require(
29          "dijit.form.TextBox");
30        dojo.require(
31          "dijit.form.Textarea");
32      </script>
33    </head>
34
35    <body class="tundra">
36      <h1>Using InlineEditBox</h1>
37      Dear
38      <span dojoType="dijit.InlineEditBox"
39        autoSave="false"
40        editor="dijit.form.TextBox">
41        [person]
42      </span>:
43      <div dojoType="dijit.InlineEditBox"
44        autoSave="false"
45        editor="dijit.form.Textarea"
46        renderAsHtml="true">
47        [Line 1]<br>
48        [Line 2]<br>
49        [Line 3]
50      </div>
```

(script continues)

Script 6.7 *continued*

```
         script

51      <div>Best wishes,</div>
52      <span dojoType="dijit.InlineEditBox"
53        autoSave="false"
54        editor="dijit.form.TextBox">
55        [Your name]
56      </span>
57    </body>
58  </html>
```

4. Save your file.

5. Navigate to your file in a browser. You should see the form letter.

6. Click the [person] text and enter a new name. A text box appears to accept the new name (**Figure 6.9**).

7. Click Save to save the name in the text of the page (**Figure 6.10**).

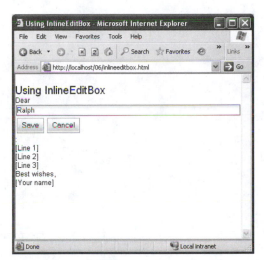

Figure 6.9 Editing text in a Web page.

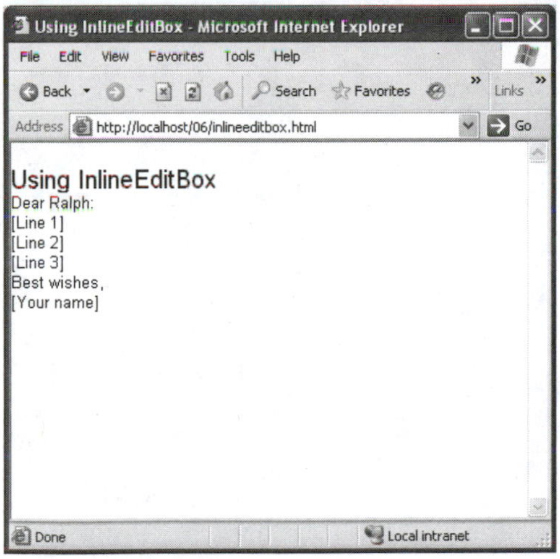

Figure 6.10 Edited text in a Web page.

Creating Tree Data

Dijit trees present the user with collapsible trees filled with items. Creating a tree takes a little work, however. You typically create a data file in JavaScript Object Notation (JSON) format, which the tree reads in to populate that tree with nodes (that is, the leaves of the tree).

The example groceries.json creates data file for a node named Groceries and gives that node five subnodes: Eggs, Spinach, and so on. You will use this data file in the task in the next section to populate a tree.

To create tree data:

1. Create a new document, groceries.json, in a text editor.

2. Add this JSON code to create the framework for the tree's data, making that data accessible under the name `'name'`:

```
{
  identifier : 'name',
  label : 'name',
  ]
}
```

3. Add this code to start listing the items in the tree:

```
{
  identifier : 'name',
  label : 'name',
  items : [
    {
    }
  ]
}
```

4. Add this code to create a Groceries node:

```
{
  identifier : 'name',
  label : 'name',
  items : [
    {
      name : 'Groceries',
    }
  ]
}
```

5. Add the child nodes (the groceries) to the Groceries node like this:

```
{
  identifier : 'name',
  label : 'name',
  items : [
    {
      name : 'Groceries',
      children: [
        {name : 'Eggs'},
        {name : 'Spinach'},
        {name : 'Hamburger'},
        {name : 'Butter'},
        {name : 'Broccoli'}
      ]
    }
  ]
}
```

6. Save your file.

You'll put this file to work in the next task.

Using Tree

You use the Tree Dijit to display a tree of collapsible nodes of data. The data for the tree is typically supplied by a `dojo.data.ItemFileReadStore` data store. Here, we'll connect our data store to the groceries.json file created in the previous task.

The example here, tree.html, displays the data in groceries.json in a tree. You can use `dojo.data.ItemFileReadStore` to read the data in from groceries.json and then connect the data store to a `dijit.tree.TreeStoreModel` Dijit, which the tree can then use to display the data.

To create a tree:

1. Open your Web page in a text editor.

2. Add `dojo.require("dijit.Tree");` and `dojo.require("dojo.data.ItemFileReadStore");` statements to your code.

3. Create a new `dojo.data.ItemFileReadStore` object and connect it to groceries.json with the `url` attribute.

4. Create a new `dijit.tree.TreeStoreModel` Dijit and connect it to the data store with the `store` and `query` attributes (use `"{name:'*'}"` as the query to select all nodes in the tree).

5. Create a new `dijit.tree.Tree` Dijit and connect it to the `dijit.tree.TreeStoreModel` Dijit with the `model` attribute.

   Script 6.8 shows what your page should look like after you make the additions.

USING TREE

Script 6.8 Creating a tree.

```
1    <html>
2      <head>
3        <title>Using Tree</title>
4
5        <link rel="stylesheet"
6          type="text/css"
7          href="http://o.aolcdn.com/
8          dojo/1.1/dojo/
9          resources/dojo.css" />
10
11       <link rel="stylesheet"
12         type="text/css"
13         href="http://o.aolcdn.com/dojo/
14         1.1/dijit/
15         themes/tundra/tundra.css" />
16
17       <script
18         djConfig="parseOnLoad:true"
19         type="text/javascript"
20         src="http://o.aolcdn.com/dojo/1.1/
21           dojo/dojo.xd.js">
22       </script>
23
24       <script type="text/javascript">
25         dojo.require("dojo.parser");
26         dojo.require(
27           "dojo.data.ItemFileReadStore");
28         dojo.require("dijit.Tree");
29       </script>
30     </head>
31
32     <body class="tundra">
33       <h1>Using Tree</h1>
34
35       <div dojoType=
36         "dojo.data.ItemFileReadStore"
37         jsId="data" url=
38         "groceries.json">
39       </div>
40
41       <div dojoType=
42         "dijit.tree.TreeStoreModel"
43         jsId="model" store="data"
44         query="{name:'*'}">
45       </div>
46
47       <div dojoType="dijit.Tree"
48         model="model">
49       </div>
50
51     </body>
52    </html>
```

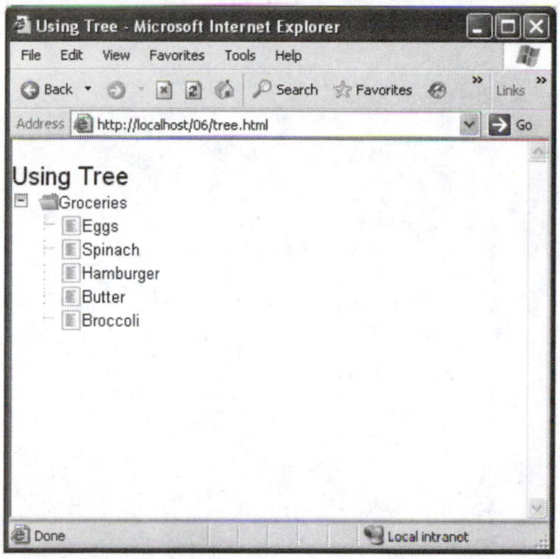

Figure 6.11 A Dijit tree.

6. Save your file.

7. Navigate to your file in a browser. You should see the new tree Dijit (**Figure 6.11**).

The Groceries node can be opened or closed (hiding the rest of the tree) by clicking it.

DRAGGING AND DROPPING

7

Dojo has built-in support for one of the most elegant Web page features: drag and drop. You might think that letting users drag and drop elements in your Web pages should be simple, but you'll find that it isn't if you write all the code yourself. After accounting for cross-browser issues, you'll be writing about five single-spaced pages of JavaScript code.

Dojo, the cross-platform JavaScript toolkit, to the rescue! Dojo has lots of drag-and-drop capability built in, and all you need to do is put it to work—which can be as easy as making the `dojoType` value of an element `dojo.dnd.Moveable` (the dnd stands for drag and drop).

In this chapter, you'll see how to add drag-and-drop capability to your Web pages, from supporting simple moveables to creating notes the user can type into and move around a Web page.

It all starts with `dojo.dnd.Moveable dojoType`. Supporting dragging and dropping can be as simple as styling the element that you want to let the user drag and drop and then setting its `dojoType` attribute to `dojo.dnd.Moveable`. We'll get started by doing exactly that.

Creating a Moveable

In Dojo, elements that can be dragged and dropped are called *moveables*. To create a moveable, you set the element's `dojoType` attribute to `dojo.dnd.Moveable`.

The example moveable.html creates and styles a moveable `<div>` element as a cyan-colored box that can be dragged around the page.

To create a moveable:

1. Open your Web page in a text editor.

2. Add a `dojo.require("dojo.dnd.Moveable");` statement to your code.

3. Create a new `<div>` element with its `class` attribute set to `"moveable"` and style it as a cyan box with a border, as shown in **Script 7.1**.

Script 7.1 Setting the class and style for a moveable.

```
1   <html>
2     <head>
3       <title>Creating a Moveable</title>
4       <style type="text/css">
5         .moveable {
6           background: cyan;
7           width: 80px;
8           height: 80px;
9           border: 1px solid black;
10          cursor: pointer;
11        }
12      </style>
13      <script
14        type="text/javascript"
15        djConfig="parseOnLoad:true"
16        src=  "http://o.aolcdn.com/
17        dojo/1.1/dojo/dojo.xd.js">
18      </script>
19
20      <script type="text/javascript">
21        dojo.require("dojo.parser");
22        dojo.require(
23          "dojo.dnd.Moveable");
24      </script>
25    </head>
26
27    <body>
28      <div class="moveable">
29      </div>
30    </body>
31  </html>
```

Script 7.2 Creating a moveable.

```
1    <html>
2      <head>
3        <title>Creating a Moveable</title>
4        <style type="text/css">
5          .moveable {
6            background: cyan;
7            width: 80px;
8            height: 80px;
9            border: 1px solid black;
10           cursor: pointer;
11         }
12       </style>
13       <script
14         type="text/javascript"
15         djConfig="parseOnLoad:true"
16         src=  "http://o.aolcdn.com/
17         dojo/1.1/dojo/dojo.xd.js">
18       </script>
19
20       <script type="text/javascript">
21         dojo.require("dojo.parser");
22         dojo.require(
23           "dojo.dnd.Moveable");
24       </script>
25     </head>
26
27     <body>
28       <h1>Creating a Moveable</h1>
29       <div class="moveable" dojoType=
30         "dojo.dnd.Moveable" >
31       </div>
32     </body>
33   </html>
```

4. Set the `<div>` element's `dojoType` attribute to `dojo.dnd.Moveable`.

   Script 7.2 shows what your page should look like after you make the additions.

5. Save your file.

6. Navigate to your file in a browser. You should see the cyan `<div>` element.

7. Drag the `<div>` element with the mouse (**Figure 7.1**).

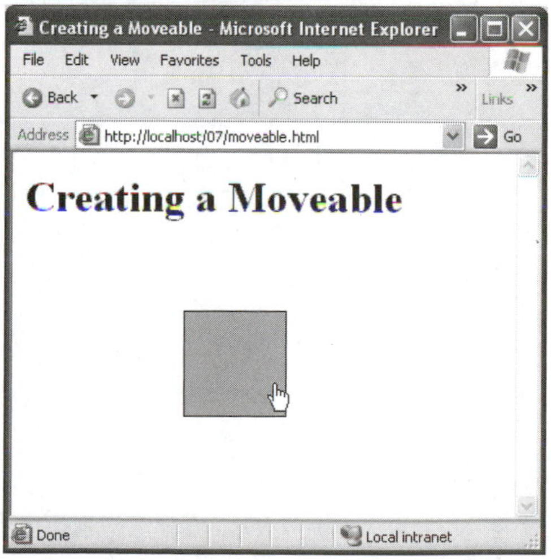

Figure 7.1 Dragging a moveable.

Creating Moveables in Code

You can also create moveables in code, which can be useful if you want to handle drag-and-drop events of the kind we'll work with later in this chapter.

The next example, moveableprogram.html, mimics the previous example, but it creates its moveable entirely in code—no <div> element needed.

To create a moveable in code:

1. Open your Web page in a text editor.

2. Add a dojo.require("dojo.dnd.Moveable"); statement to your code.

3. Create a new <div> element with its class attribute set to "moveable" and style it as a cyan box with a border, as shown in **Script 7.3**.

Script 7.3 Setting the class and style for a moveable.

```
1    <html>
2      <head>
3        <title>Creating a Moveable in
4          Code</title>
5        <style type="text/css">
6          .moveable {
7            background: cyan;
8            width: 80px;
9            height: 80px;
10           cursor: pointer;
11           border: 1px solid black;
12         }
13       </style>
14       <script
15         type="text/javascript"
16         djConfig="parseOnLoad:true"
17         src="http://o.aolcdn.com/
18           dojo/1.1/dojo/dojo.xd.js">
19       </script>
20
21       <script type="text/javascript">
22         dojo.require("dojo.parser");
23         dojo.require("dojo.dnd.Moveable");
24       </script>
25     </head>
26
27     <body>
28       <h1>Creating a Moveable in Code</h1>
29     </body>
30   </html>
```

Script 7.4 Creating a moveable in code.

```
1   <html>
2     <head>
3       <title>Creating a Moveable in
4         Code</title>
5       <style type="text/css">
6         .moveable {
7           background: cyan;
8           width: 80px;
9           height: 80px;
10          cursor: pointer;
11          border: 1px solid black;
12        }
13      </style>
14      <script
15        type="text/javascript"
16        djConfig="parseOnLoad:true"
17        src="http://o.aolcdn.com/
18          dojo/1.1/dojo/dojo.xd.js">
19      </script>
20      <script type="text/javascript">
21        dojo.require("dojo.parser");
22        dojo.require("dojo.dnd.Moveable");
23        dojo.addOnLoad(function() {
24          var div =
25            document.createElement("div");
26          dojo.addClass(div, "moveable");
27          dojo.body().appendChild(div);
28          var moveable = new
29            dojo.dnd.Moveable(div);
30        });
31      </script>
32    </head>
33    <body>
34      <h1>Creating a Moveable in Code</h1>
35    </body>
36  </html>
```

4. In an `addOnLoad` function, create a new `<div>` element. Add the `moveable` class to the new `<div>` element and append the `<div>` element to the Web page.

5. Make the `<div>` element a `dojo.dnd.Moveable` element.

Script 7.4 shows what your page should look like after you make the additions.

6. Save your file.

7. Navigate to your file in a browser. You should see the new moveable (**Figure 7.2**).

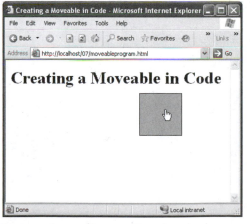

Figure 7.2 A moveable created in code.

Adding Dijits to Moveables

Dragging a <div> element around is fun, but you can display an element, such as a text area, in a moveable as well.

The example note.html creates a moveable text area that the user can drag around the page and type in.

To create a moveable text area:

1. Open your Web page in a text editor.

2. Add a dojo.require("dojo.dnd. Moveable"); statement to your code.

3. Create a new <div> element with its class attribute set to "moveable" and style it as a cyan box with a border, as shown in **Script 7.5**.

Script 7.5 Setting the class and style for a moveable text area.

```
1   <html>
2     <head>
3       <title>Adding Dijits to
4         Moveables</title>
5       <style type="text/css">
6         .moveable {
7           background: cyan;
8           border: 1px solid black;
9           width: 80px;
10          height: 80px;
11        }
12      </style>
13
14      <script
15        type="text/javascript"
16        djConfig="parseOnLoad:true"
17        src="http://o.aolcdn.com/
18          dojo/1.1/dojo/dojo.xd.js">
19      </script>
20
21      <script type="text/javascript">
22        dojo.require("dojo.parser");
23        dojo.require(
24          "dojo.dnd.Moveable");
25      </script>
26    </head>
27
28    <body>
29      <h1>Adding Dijits to Moveables</h1>
30
31      <div dojoType="dojo.dnd.Moveable">
32      </div>
33    </body>
34  </html>
```

Script 7.6 Creating a moveable text area.

```
1    <html>
2      <head>
3        <title>Adding Dijits to
4          Moveables</title>
5        <style type="text/css">
6          .moveable {
7            background: cyan;
8            border: 1px solid black;
9            width: 80px;
10           height: 80px;
11         }
12       </style>
13
14       <script
15         type="text/javascript"
16         djConfig="parseOnLoad:true"
17        src="http://o.aolcdn.com/
18          dojo/1.1/dojo/dojo.xd.js">
19       </script>
20
21       <script type="text/javascript">
22         dojo.require("dojo.parser");
23         dojo.require(
24           "dojo.dnd.Moveable");
25       </script>
26     </head>
27
28     <body>
29       <h1>Adding Dijits to Moveables</h1>
30
31       <div dojoType="dojo.dnd.Moveable">
32         <textarea class="moveable">
33           Enter your text!
34         </textarea>
35       </div>
36     </body>
37   </html>
```

4. Insert a text area into the moveable, as shown in **Script 7.6**.

5. Save your file.

6. Navigate to your file in a browser. You should see the draggable text area.

7. Enter text in the text area. You should see your text appear in the draggable text area (**Figure 7.3**).

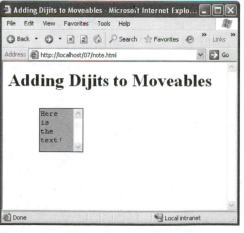

Figure 7.3 Entering text in a draggable text area.

Using Draggable Handles

The previous task showed how to make a text area draggable, but that's not always what you want. What if the user drags the mouse to try to select text? As things stand, the whole text area would move. You can fix this problem by adding a dragging handle.

The example notehandle.html adds a handle above the text area and disables the text area's ability to start dragging operations.

To create a draggable handle:

1. Open your Web page in a text editor.

2. Add a `dojo.require("dojo.dnd.Moveable");` statement to your code.

3. Create two new `style` classes, one for the moveable text area and a smaller one for the dragging handle, as shown in **Script 7.7**.

Script 7.7 Creating style classes for a moveable with a draggable handle.

```
1    <html>
2      <head>
3        <title>Using Handles with
4          Moveables</title>
5        <style type="text/css">
6          .moveable {
7            background: cyan;
8            border: 1px solid black;
9            width: 80px;
10           height: 80px;}
11          .draggable {
12            border: 1px solid black;
13            cursor: pointer;
14            background: cyan;
15            width : 80px;
16            height: 10px;}
17       </style>
18       <script type="text/javascript"
19         djConfig="parseOnLoad:true"
20         src="http://o.aolcdn.com/
21           dojo/1.1/dojo/dojo.xd.js">
22       </script>
23       <script type="text/javascript">
24         dojo.require("dojo.parser");
25         dojo.require("dojo.dnd.Moveable");
26       </script>
27     </head>
28     <body>
29       <h1>Using Handles with Moveables</h1>
30     </body>
31   </html>
```

Script 7.8 Creating a draggable handle.

```
1    <html>
2      <head>
3        <title>Using Handles with
4          Moveables</title>
5        <style type="text/css">
6          .moveable {
7            background: cyan;
8            border: 1px solid black;
9            width: 80px;
10           height: 80px;
11         }
12         .draggable {
13           border: 1px solid black;
14           cursor: pointer;
15           background: cyan;
16           width : 80px;
17           height: 10px;
18         }
19       </style>
20       <script type="text/javascript"
21         djConfig="parseOnLoad:true"
22         src="http://o.aolcdn.com/
23           dojo/1.1/dojo/dojo.xd.js">
24       </script>
25       <script type="text/javascript">
26         dojo.require("dojo.parser");
27         dojo.require("dojo.dnd.Moveable");
28       </script>
29     </head>
30     <body>
31       <h1>Using Handles with Moveables</h1>
32       <div dojoType="dojo.dnd.Moveable"
33         handle="handle">
34         <div id="handle"
35           class="draggable"></div>
36         <textarea class="moveable">Enter
37           your text!
38         </textarea>
39       </div>
40     </body>
41   </html>
```

4. Add the dragging handle to the moveable `<div>` element, setting the `<div>` element's `handle` attribute to the handle's ID, as shown in **Script 7.8**.

5. Save your file.

6. Navigate to your file in a browser and enter text in the text area (**Figure 7.4**). Then try dragging the box.

Note that you need to drag using the dragging handle at the top, not the text area.

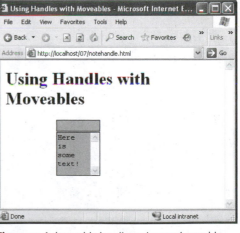

Figure 7.4 A draggable handle and a nondraggable text area.

Responding to Drag Events

You can also make your dragged items respond to drag events, such as the starting and stopping of dragging.

The next example, moveableevents.html, catches the start of a drag operation and turns the text area in the draggable <div> blue.

To respond to drag events:

1. Open your Web page in a text editor.

2. Add a dojo.require("dojo.dnd.Moveable"); statement to your code.

3. Create a new style, dragging, that includes a blur background.

4. Use the dojo.subscribe method to connect code to the "/dnd/move/start" and "/dnd/move/stop" events, and use dojo.query to add and remove the dragging class to and from the text area when dragging starts and stops.

   Script 7.9 shows what your page should look like after you make the additions.

Script 7.9 Responding to drag events.

```
1    <html>
2      <head>
3        <title>Responding to Drag
4        Events</title>
5        <style type="text/css">
6          .moveable {
7            background: cyan;
8            border: 1px solid black;
9            width: 80px;
10           height: 80px;
11         }
12         .draggable {
13           border: 1px solid black;
14           cursor :pointer;
15           background: cyan;
16           width : 80px;
17           height: 10px;
18         }
19         .dragging {
20           background : blue;
21         }
22       </style>
23
24       <script
25         type="text/javascript"
26         djConfig="parseOnLoad:true"
27         src="http://o.aolcdn.com/
28         dojo/1.1/dojo/dojo.xd.js">
29       </script>
30
31       <script type="text/javascript">
32         dojo.require("dojo.parser");
33         dojo.require(
34           "dojo.dnd.Moveable");
35         dojo.addOnLoad(function() {
36         dojo.subscribe(
37           "/dnd/move/start", function(n){
38           dojo.query("#moveable >
39           textarea").addClass("dragging");
40         });
41         dojo.subscribe(
```

(script continues)

Script 7.9 *continued*

```
42        "/dnd/move/stop", function(n){
43        dojo.query("#moveable >
44       textarea").removeClass(
45       "dragging");
46       });
47    });
48    </script>
49   </head>
50
51   <body>
52    <h1>Responding to Drag Events</h1>
53
54    <div id="moveable"
55     dojoType="dojo.dnd.Moveable"
56     handle="handle">
57     <div id="handle"
58       class="draggable"></div>
59     <textarea class="moveable">Enter
60       your text!</textarea>
61    </div>
62   </body>
63  </html>
```

5. Save your file.

6. Navigate to your file in a browser and drag the handle. You should see the text area turn blue (**Figure 7.5**).

Figure 7.5 Responding to a drag start event.

Using Multiple Moveables

When you have multiple moveables on a Web page, you have to arrange them so that when the user drags one, it doesn't slide under other elements as the user moves it. The way to do that is to give the dragged element a higher HTML z-index value than the other elements.

The example sindex.html has two moveables. When the user starts dragging one, that moveable is given a higher z-index value than the other, so that the dragged moveable always rides over the stationary one.

To keep the dragged movable visible when using multiple moveables:

1. Open your Web page in a text editor.

2. Add a `dojo.require("dojo.dnd.Moveable");` statement to your code.

3. Create two new moveables and use the `dojo.connect` method to connect a function to their `onMoveStart` events that uses the `dojo.style` method to increase the z-index value.

   Script 7.10 shows what your page should look like after you make the additions.

Script 7.10 Keeping the dragged movable visible when using multiple moveables.

```
1   <html>
2     <head>
3       <title>Setting Z-Index</title>
4       <style type="text/css">
5         .moveable {
6           background: cyan;
7           border: 1px solid black;
8           width: 80px;
9           height: 80px;
10        }
11        .draggable {
12          border: 1px solid black;
13          cursor :pointer;
14          background: cyan;
15          width : 80px;
16          height: 10px;
17        }
18      </style>
19      <script type="text/javascript"
20        src="http://o.aolcdn.com/
21        dojo/1.1/dojo/dojo.xd.js">
22      </script>
23
24      <script type="text/javascript">
25        dojo.require(
26          "dojo.dnd.Moveable");
27
28        dojo.addOnLoad(function() {
29          var moveable1 = new
30          dojo.dnd.Moveable("moveable1",
31          {handle : "handle1"});
32          var moveable2 = new
33          dojo.dnd.Moveable("moveable2",
34          {handle : "handle2"});
35
36          var zIndex = 0;
37          dojo.connect(moveable1,
38            "onMoveStart", function(mover){
39              dojo.style(mover.host.node,
40              "zIndex", zIndex++);
41          });
42          dojo.connect(moveable2,
43            "onMoveStart", function(mover){
44              dojo.style(mover.host.node,
45              "zIndex", zIndex++);
```

(script continues)

Script 7.10 *continued*

```
                    script
46          });
47        });
48      </script>
49   </head>
50
51   <body>
52     <h1>Setting Z-Index</h1>
53     <div id="moveable1"
54       dojoType="dojo.dnd.Moveable">
55       <div id='handle1'
56         class="draggable"></div>
57       <textarea class"moveable">Here is
58         some text</textarea>
59     </div>
60     <div id="moveable2"
61       dojoType="dojo.dnd.Moveable">
62       <div id='handle2'
63         class="draggable"></div>
64       <textarea class="moveable">Here is
65         more text</textarea>
66     </div>
67   </body>
68 </html>
```

4. Save your file.

5. Navigate to your file in a browser. You should two moveables (**Figure 7.6**).

6. Drag one to watch it ride over the other (**Figure 7.7**).

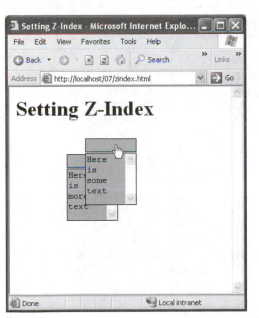

Figure 7.6 Two moveables.

Figure 7.7 One moveable riding over the other.

Setting Motion Limits

Dojo lets you limit where an element can be dragged. You limit the drag motion with the `constraints` item when calling the `dojo.dnd.move.constrainedMoveable` constructor.

The example limits.html limits one moveable to a box with a size of 200 x 200 pixels.

To limit drag motion:

1. Open your Web page in a text editor.

2. Add `dojo.require("dojo.dnd.Moveable");` and `dojo.require("dojo.dnd.move");` statements to your code.

3. Create two new moveables. For one, specify `dojo.dnd.move.constrainedMoveable` and set the `contraints` item to a box of 200 x 200 pixels.

   Script 7.11 shows what your page should look like after you make the additions.

Script 7.11 Limiting drag motion.

```
1   <html>
2     <head>
3       <title>Setting Drag Limits</title>
4       <style type="text/css">
5         .moveable {
6           background: cyan;
7           border: 1px solid black;
8           width: 80px;
9           height: 80px;
10        }
11        .draggable {
12          border: 1px solid black;
13          cursor :pointer;
14          background: cyan;
15          width : 80px;
16          height: 10px;
17        }
18      </style>
19      <script type="text/javascript"
20        src="http://o.aolcdn.com/
21        dojo/1.1/dojo/dojo.xd.js">
22      </script>
23      <script type="text/javascript">
24        dojo.require("dojo.dnd.Moveable");
25        dojo.require("dojo.dnd.move");
26
27        dojo.addOnLoad(function() {
28          var limits = function() {
29            box = {};
30            box["t"] = 0;
31            box["l"] = 0;
32            box["w"] = 200;
33            box["h"] = 200;
34            return box;
35          }
36          var moveable1 = new
37          dojo.dnd.move
38          .constrainedMoveable("moveable1",
39          {handle : "handle1", constraints
40          : limits, within : true});
41          var moveable2 = new
42          dojo.dnd.Moveable("moveable2",
43          {handle : "handle2"});
44          var zIndex = 0;
45          dojo.connect(moveable1,
```

(script continues)

Script 7.11 *continued*

```
                        script
46          "onMoveStart", function(mover){
47            dojo.style(mover.host.node,
48            "zIndex", zIndex++);
49          });
50          dojo.connect(moveable2,
51            "onMoveStart", function(mover){
52            dojo.style(mover.host.node,
53            "zIndex", zIndex++);
54          });
55        });
56      </script>
57    </head>
58    <body>
59      <h1>Setting Drag Limits</h1>
60      <div id="moveable1">
61        <div id='handle1'
62          class="draggable"></div>
63        <textarea class="moveable">Here is
64          some text</textarea>
65      </div>
66      <div id="moveable2">
67        <div id='handle2'
68          class="draggable"></div>
69        <textarea class="moveable">Here is
70          more text</textarea>
71      </div>
72    </body>
73  </html>
```

4. Save your file.

5. Navigate to your file in a browser and drag the first moveable. You should see it stop at the borders of a 200 x 200 box (**Figure 7.8**).

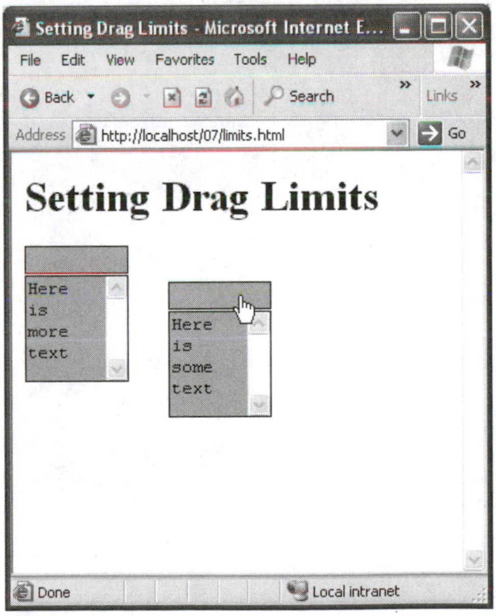

Figure 7.8 Constrained dragging.

Using Source to Drag HTML Elements

Dojo comes with a package named dojo.dnd. Source that lets you drag HTML elements on Web pages. When you use dojo.dnd.Source, you give the enclosed draggable elements the dojoType attribute "dojoDndItem".

This example, source.html, lets the user drag and rearrange some text in a page.

To use Source to drag elements:

1. Open your Web page in a text editor.

2. Add a dojo.require("dojo.dnd.Source"); statement to your code.

3. Create a new <div> element with dojoType set to dojo.dnd.Source and four <div> elements enclosing text inside it, with class set to dojoDndItem.

   Script 7.12 shows what your page should look like after you make the additions.

Script 7.12 Using Source to drag elements.

```
1   <html>
2     <head>
3       <title>Using Source</title>
4
5       <link rel="stylesheet"
6         type="text/css"
7         href="http://o.aolcdn.com/dojo/1.1/
8         dijit/themes/tundra/tundra.css" />
9
10      <link rel="stylesheet"
11        type="text/css"
12        href="http://o.aolcdn.com/
13        dojo/1.1/dojo/resources/dojo.css"
14        />
15
16      <link rel="stylesheet"
17        type="text/css"
18        href="http://o.aolcdn.com/
19        dojo/1.1/dojo/resources/dnd.css" />
20
21      <script
22        type="text/javascript"
23        djConfig="parseOnLoad:true"
24        src="http://o.aolcdn.com/
25          dojo/1.1/dojo/dojo.xd.js">
26      </script>
27
28      <script type="text/javascript">
29        dojo.require("dojo.parser");
30        dojo.require("dojo.dnd.Source");
31      </script>
32
33    </head>
34    <body>
35      <h1>Using Source</h1>
36      <br>
37
38      <div dojoType="dojo.dnd.Source"
39        class="container">
40
41        <div class="dojoDndItem">
```

(script continues)

Script 7.12 *continued*

```
          script
42              <b>First</b></div>
43
44        <div class="dojoDndItem">
45          <b>Second</b></div>
46
47        <div class="dojoDndItem">
48          <b>Third</b></div>
49
50        <div class="dojoDndItem">
51          <b>Fourth</b></div>
52
53        </div>
54     </body>
55   </html>
```

4. Save your file.

5. Navigate to your file in a browser and drag the text "Third." You should see an insertion arrow appear (**Figure 7.9**).

6. Drop the "Third" item so that it appears first. The text should be rearranged (**Figure 7.10**).

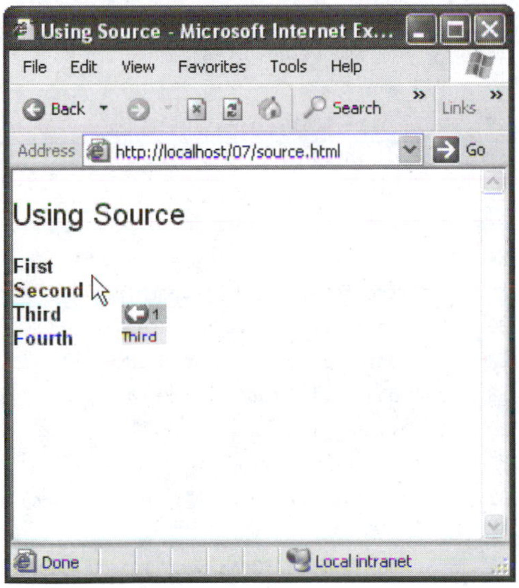

Figure 7.9 Dragging an item.

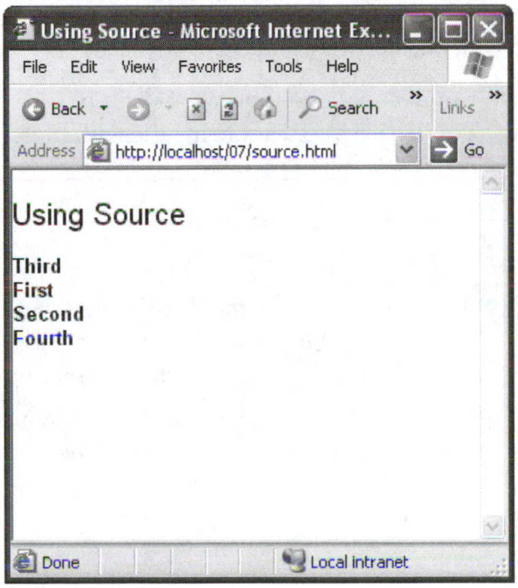

Figure 7.10 The rearranged text.

Chapter 7

Handling Events with Source

You can also handle drag-and-drop events when using dojo.dnd.Source. Just use dojo.subscribe to connect a function to the events that you want to handle.

The example drop.html displays an alert box when the user drops an element.

To handle events with Source:

1. Open your Web page in a text editor.

2. Add a dojo.require("dojo.dnd.Source"); statement to your code.

3. Create a new <div> element with dojoType set to dojo.dnd.Source and four <div> elements enclosing text inside it, with class set to dojoDndItem.

4. Connect code to the drag-and-drop events that you want to handle with the dojo.subscribe method.

✔ Tip

■ In the script here, the code for all but the drop event is commented out so that you don't have to click a lot of OK buttons in alert boxes as you drag and drop elements. Script 7.13 shows what your page should look like after you make the additions.

Script 7.13 Handling events with Source.

```
1   <html>
2     <head>
3       <title>Handling Drop Events</title>
4         <link rel="stylesheet"
5           type="text/css"
6           href="http://o.aolcdn.com/
7           dojo/1.1/dijit/themes/
8           tundra/tundra.css" />
9         <link rel="stylesheet"
10          type="text/css"
11          href="http://o.aolcdn.com/
12          dojo/1.1/dojo/resources/
13          dojo.css" />
14        <link rel="stylesheet"
15          type="text/css"
16          href="http://o.aolcdn.com/
17          dojo/1.1/dojo/tests/
18          dnd/dndDefault.css" />
19        <script
20          type="text/javascript"
21          djConfig="parseOnLoad:true"
22          src="http://o.aolcdn.com/
23            dojo/1.1/dojo/dojo.xd.js">
24        </script>
25        <script type="text/javascript">
26          dojo.require("dojo.parser");
27          dojo.require("dojo.dnd.Source");
28          dojo.addOnLoad(function()
29          {
30            dojo.subscribe(
31            "/dnd/source/over", function(src)
32            {
33              //alert("Drag over");
34            });
35            dojo.subscribe("/dnd/start",
36            function(src, nodes, copy)
37              //alert("Drag start");
38            });
39            dojo.subscribe("/dnd/drop",
40            function(src, nodes, copy)
41            {
42              alert("Drop");
```

(script continues)

Script 7.13 continued

```
43          });
44          dojo.subscribe("/dnd/cancel",
45          function()
46          {
47            //alert("Drag cancel");
48          });
49        });
50      </script>
51    </head>
52    <body>
53      <h1>Handling Drop Events</h1>
54      <br>
55      <div dojoType="dojo.dnd.Source"
56        class="container">
57        <div class="dojoDndItem">
58          <b>First</b></div>
59        <div class="dojoDndItem">
60          <b>Second</b></div>
61        <div class="dojoDndItem">
62          <b>Third</b></div>
63        <div class="dojoDndItem">
64          <b>Fourth</b></div>
65      </div>
66    </body>
67  </html>
```

5. Save your file.

6. Navigate to your file in a browser and drag and then drop an element. When you drop the element, an alert box appears indicating that the drop took place (**Figure 7.11**).

Figure 7.11 Catching a drop event.

ANIMATION AND SPECIAL EFFECTS

Dojo supports animation, as you'll see in this chapter.

You can use animation to make elements fade out, or slide to a new location, or wipe to invisibility. You can also use animation to expand the size of elements when they're clicked, display and fade out an image with drag-and-drop operations, and toggle elements from visible to hidden. You can even use animation to create blended colors. These effects are unexpected in Web pages, so they make your pages stand out.

Chapter 8

Using Fades

You can use the dojo.fadeOut method to make elements fade out as the user watches. This effect is purely visual—the elements are still there, just invisible.

The example fade.html displays a <div> element with some text and an HTML text field. When you click the <div> element, it fades out, along with its enclosed text and text field. The <div> element and text field are actually still there, as you can verify by clicking the (invisible) text field; you'll see the mouse pointer change to a text-insertion cursor.

To make elements fade out:

1. Open your Web page in a text editor.

2. Create a <div> element with the ID "div" that's styled in cyan and encloses a text field.

3. Connect code in an addOnLoad function to call the dojo.fadeOut method when the <div> element is clicked.

4. Use the play method to execute the animation.

   Script 8.1 shows how your page should look after you make the additions.

Script 8.1 Making elements fade out.

```
1    <html>
2      <head>
3
4        <title>Using Fades</title>
5
6        <link rel="stylesheet"
7          type="text/css" href=
8          "http://o.aolcdn.com/dojo/1.1/
9          dojo/resources/dojo.css" />
10
11       <link rel="stylesheet"
12         type="text/css"
13         href="http://o.aolcdn.com/
14         dojo/1.1/dijit/themes/
15         tundra/tundra.css" />
16
17       <style type="text/css">
18         .div {
19           height : 100px;
20           width : 100px;
21           background : cyan;
22         }
23       </style>
24
25       <script
26         type="text/javascript"
27         src="http://o.aolcdn.com/dojo/1.1/
28         dojo/dojo.xd.js">
29       </script>
30
31       <script type="text/javascript">
32         dojo.addOnLoad(function( ) {
33         var div = dojo.byId("div");
34         dojo.connect(div, "onclick",
35         function(evt) {
36           var animated = dojo.fadeOut({
37           node : div});
38           animated.play();
39         });
40       });
41       </script>
42     </head>
```

(script continues)

Script 8.1 *continued*

```
43
44    <body>
45      <h1>Using Fades</h1>
46
47      <div id="div" class="div">
48        <h1>Click me</h1>
49        <input type="text"
50        value="hello"></input>
51      </div>
52
53    </body>
54  </html>
```

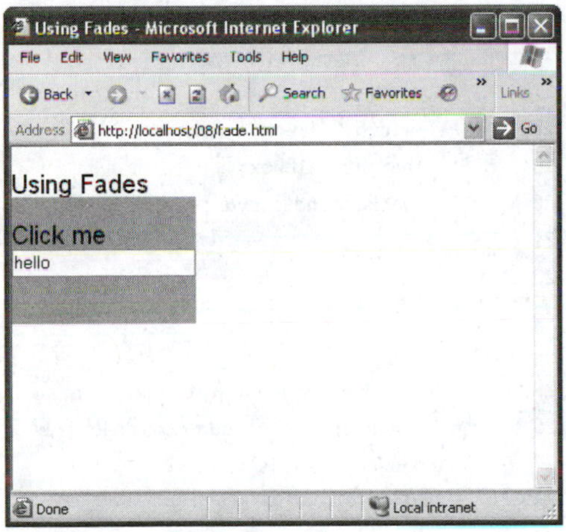

Figure 8.1 The fadeable <div> element.

5. Save your file.

6. Navigate to your file in a browser; you should see the <div> element and the text field (**Figure 8.1**).

7. Click the <div> element. You will see it fade out—the text, colored <div> element, and the text field all disappear.

✔ Tips

■ You can specify the duration of the transition with the `duration` parameter (measured in milliseconds). See the next task for details.

■ You can also make elements fade in, using the `fadeIn` method.

Controlling Fade Speed with Functions

You can control how a fade proceeds—that is, how slowly or quickly. You do that with *easing functions*; the animation then follows the form of that function. For example, if you use an easing function with a curve that stays flat and then rises suddenly, your fade-out operation will proceed slowly until the very end; then it will conclude rapidly.

The example here, fadefunction.html, uses a fadeout function with a curve that rises rapidly at the end, making the fade conclude quickly.

To use easing functions to control fade speed:

1. Open your Web page in a text editor.

2. Create a <div> element with the ID "div" that's styled in cyan and encloses a text field.

3. Create an easing function, such as $f(t) = t^3$ here.

   This function creates a curve that starts flat and then rises suddenly, so your transition will start slowly and then finish rapidly.

4. Connect code in an addOnLoad function to call the dojo.fadeOut method when the <div> element is clicked, pass the easing function to the dojo.fadeOut method, and set the duration parameter to 1000 milliseconds (that is, 1 second).

5. Use the play method to execute the animation.

   Script 8.2 shows how your page should look after you make the additions.

Script 8.2 Using easing functions to control fade speed.

```
1   <html>
2     <head>
3      <title>Using Fade Functions</title>
4
5       <link rel="stylesheet"
6         type="text/css" href=
7         "http://o.aolcdn.com/dojo/1.1/
8         dojo/resources/dojo.css" />
9
10      <link rel="stylesheet"
11        type="text/css"
12        href="http://o.aolcdn.com/
13        dojo/1.1/dijit/themes/
14        tundra/tundra.css" />
15
16     <style type="text/css">
17       .div {
18         width : 100px;
19         height : 100px;
20         background : cyan;
21       }
22     </style>
23
24     <script
25       type="text/javascript"
26       src="http://o.aolcdn.com/dojo/1.1/
27       dojo/dojo.xd.js">
28     </script>
29
30     <script type="text/javascript">
31       dojo.addOnLoad(function() {
32       var div = dojo.byId("div");
33       dojo.connect(div, "onclick",
34         function(evt) {
35         var easingFunction = function(t)
36         {
37           return t * t * t;
38         }
39         dojo.fadeOut({
40           node:div,
41           easing : easingFunction,
```

(script continues)

Script 8.2 *continued*

```
42          duration : 1000
43       }).play();
44     });
45   });
46   </script>
47 </head>
48
49 <body>
50   <h1>Using Fade Functions</h1>
51
52   <div id="div"
53     class="div"><h1>Click me</h1>
54     <input type="text"
55     value="hello"></input>
56   </div>
57 </body>
58 </html>
```

6. Save your file.

7. Navigate to your file in a browser; you should see the <div> element and the text field (**Figure 8.2**).

8. Click the <div> element. You will see it fade out: slowly at first, and then rapidly.

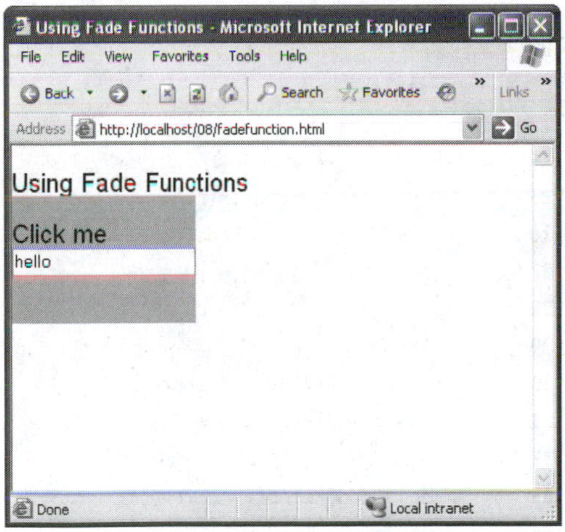

Figure 8.2 The fadeable <div> element with an easing function to control fade speed.

Sliding Elements

You can use the `dojo.fx.slideTo` method to slide elements to a new position in a Web page. To use this method, you pass the element you want to slide and the new top and left positions. The element will slide visually when you call the `play` method.

The example slider.html displays a `<div>` element containing some text and an HTML text field; the `<div>` element slides when you click it.

To slide an element:

1. Open your Web page in a text editor.

2. Add a `dojo.require("dojo.fx")`; statement to your code.

3. Create a `<div>` element with the ID "`div`" that's styled in cyan and encloses a text field.

4. Connect code in an `addOnLoad` function to call the `dojo.slideTo` method when the `<div>` element is clicked.

5. Use the `play` method to execute the animation.

   Script 8.3 shows how your page should look after you make the additions.

Script 8.3 Sliding an element.

```
1   <html>
2     <head>
3       <title>Sliding Elements</title>
4
5       <link rel="stylesheet"
6         type="text/css" href=
7         "http://o.aolcdn.com/dojo/1.1/
8         dojo/resources/dojo.css" />
9
10      <link rel="stylesheet"
11        type="text/css"
12        href="http://o.aolcdn.com/
13        dojo/1.1/dijit/themes/
14        tundra/tundra.css" />
15
16    <style type="text/css">
17      .div {
18        height : 100px;
19        width : 100px;
20        background : cyan;
21      }
22    </style>
23
24    <script
25      type="text/javascript"
26      src="http://o.aolcdn.com/
27      dojo/1.1/dojo/dojo.xd.js">
28    </script>
29
30    <script type="text/javascript">
31      dojo.require("dojo.fx");
32
33      dojo.addOnLoad(function() {
34      var div = dojo.byId("div");
35      dojo.connect(div, "onclick",
36        function(evt) {
37        dojo.fx.slideTo({
38          node:div,
39          top : "100",
40          left : "100"
41        }).play();
42      });
```

(script continues)

Script 8.3 *continued*

```
○ ○ ○                    script
43          });
44       </script>
45     </head>
46
47     <body>
48       <h1>Sliding Elements</h1>
49
50       <div id="div" class="div">
51         <h1>Click me</h1>
52         <input type="text"
53           value="hello"></input>
54       </div>
55     </body>
56   </html>
```

6. Save your file.

7. Navigate to your file in a browser.

8. Click the <div> element to make it slide to a new location (**Figure 8.3**).

✔ Tip

- You might use this animation, for example, to show how some process consisting of stages works, arranging the various steps in response to button clicks.

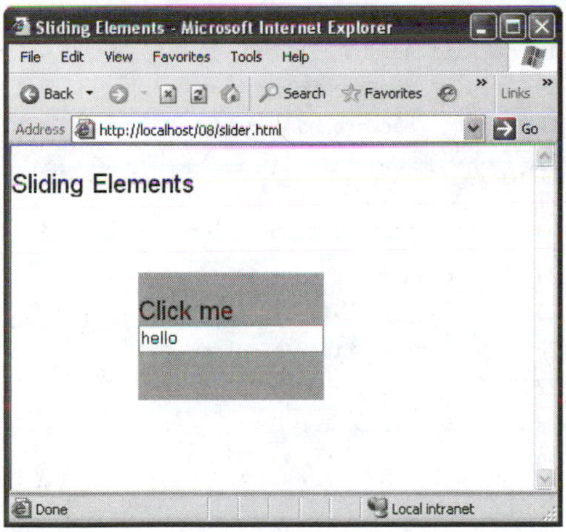

Figure 8.3 The <div> element after it has slid.

Wiping Elements

You can use the `dojo.fx.wipeOut` method to wipe elements into invisibility. The element will be wiped visually when you call the `play` method.

The example wiper.html displays a `<div>` element containing some text and an HTML text field; the `<div>` element is wiped out visually when you click it. The wiping always proceeds from the bottom up.

To wipe elements:

1. Open your Web page in a text editor.

2. Add a `dojo.require("dojo.fx");` statement to your code.

3. Create a `<div>` element with the ID `"div"` that's styled in cyan and encloses a text field.

4. Connect code in an `addOnLoad` function to call the `dojo.wipeOut` method when the `<div>` element is clicked.

5. Use the `play` method to execute the animation.

   Script 8.4 shows how your page should look after you make the additions.

Script 8.4 Wiping elements.

```
1    <html>
2      <head>
3      <title>Wiping Elements</title>
4
5      <link rel="stylesheet"
6        type="text/css" href=
7        "http://o.aolcdn.com/dojo/1.1/
8        dojo/resources/dojo.css" />
9
10     <link rel="stylesheet"
11       type="text/css"
12       href="http://o.aolcdn.com/
13       dojo/1.1/dijit/themes/
14       tundra/tundra.css" />
15
16     <style type="text/css">
17       .div {
18         height : 100px;
19         width : 100px;
20         background : cyan;
21       }
22     </style>
23
24     <script
25       type="text/javascript"
26       src="http://o.aolcdn.com/
27       dojo/1.1/dojo/dojo.xd.js">
28     </script>
29
30     <script type="text/javascript">
31       dojo.require("dojo.fx");
32
33       dojo.addOnLoad(function() {
34       var div = dojo.byId("div");
35       dojo.connect(div, "onclick",
36         function(evt) {
37         dojo.fx.wipeOut({
38           node:div
39         }).play();
40         });
41       });
42     </script>
```

(script continues)

Script 8.4 *continued*

```
                    script
43      </head>
44
45      <body>
46        <h1>Wiping Elements</h1>
47
48        <div id="div" class="div">
49          <h1>Click me</h1>
50          <input type="text"
51            value="hello"></input>
52        </div>
53      </body>
54    </html>
```

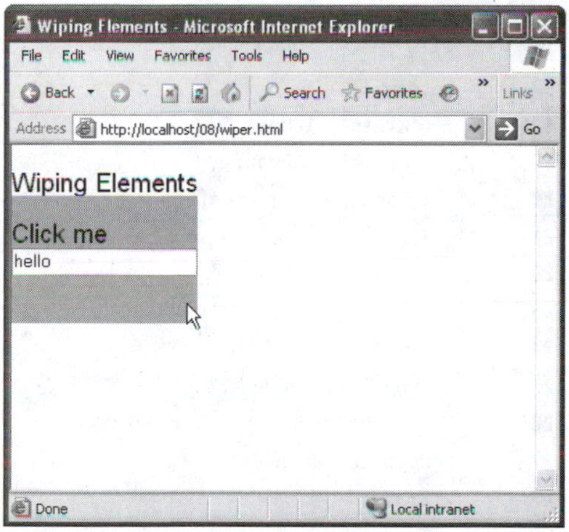

Figure 8.4 A wipeable <div> element.

6. Save your file.

7. Navigate to your file in a browser (**Figure 8.4**).

8. Click the <div> element to wipe it into invisibility, proceeding from bottom to top.

✔ Tip

■ You might use this animation, for example, to uncover a hidden element in response to the user's supplying some data or logging in.

Expanding Elements

You can use the `dojo.animateProperty` method to expand elements by supplying a beginning and ending height and width for the element.

The example expander.html displays a `<div>` element containing some text and an HTML text field; the `<div>` element expands when you click it.

To expand elements:

1. Open your Web page in a text editor.

2. Create a `<div>` element with the ID `"div"` that's styled in cyan and encloses a text field.

3. Connect code in an `addOnLoad` function to call the `dojo.animateProperty` method when the `<div>` element is clicked.

4. Set the `start` and `end` values for the `height` and `width` properties to specify how the expansion should proceed.

5. Use the `play` method to execute the animation.

   Script 8.5 shows how your page should look after you make the additions.

Script 8.5 Expanding elements.

```
1   <html>
2    <head>
3     <title>Expanding Elements</title>
4
5     <link rel="stylesheet"
6       type="text/css" href=
7       "http://o.aolcdn.com/dojo/1.1/
8       dojo/resources/dojo.css" />
9
10    <link rel="stylesheet"
11      type="text/css"
12      href="http://o.aolcdn.com/
13      dojo/1.1/dijit/themes/
14      tundra/tundra.css" />
15
16    <style type="text/css">
17     .div {
18       width : 100px;
19       height : 100px;
20       background : cyan;
21     }
22    </style>
23
24    <script
25      type="text/javascript"
26      src="http://o.aolcdn.com/
27      dojo/1.1/dojo/dojo.xd.js">
28    </script>
29
30    <script type="text/javascript">
31      dojo.addOnLoad(function() {
32      var div = dojo.byId("div");
33      dojo.connect(div, "onclick",
34        function(evt) {
35      dojo.animateProperty({
36        node : div,
37        duration : 1000,
38        properties : {
39          height : {start : '100',
40          end : '200'},
41          width : {start : '100',
42          end : '200'}
```

(script continues)

Script 8.5 *continued*

```
                script
43              }
44          }).play();
45          });
46      });
47      </script>
48  </head>
49
50  <body>
51      <h1>Expanding Elements</h1>
52
53      <div id="div" class="div">
54        <h1>Click me</h1>
55        <input type="text"
56          value="hello"></input>
57      </div>
58  </body>
59  </html>
```

6. Save your file.

7. Navigate to your file in a browser.

8. Click the <div> element to make it expand—in this case, doubling its size in both dimensions (**Figure 8.5**).

✔ Tip

■ You can make elements contract instead of expand by specifying a smaller width and height as the end points of the animation.

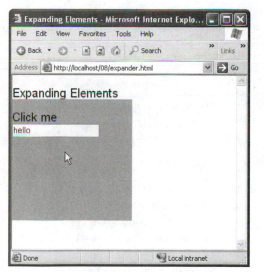

Figure 8.5 The expanded <div> element.

Controlling Expansion Speed with Functions

You can expand elements using easing functions to control the rate at which they expand. For instance, the curve of an easing function of $f(t) = t^3$ rises rapidly—the larger the value of t, the more rapidly the curve rises—so the expansion proceeds slowly at first and then more rapidly toward the end.

The example expanderfunction.html uses the easing function $f(t) = t^3$ to expand the `<div>` element slowly at first and then more rapidly at the end.

To expand elements with easing functions:

1. Open your Web page in a text editor.

2. Create a `<div>` element with the ID "div" that's styled in cyan and encloses a text field.

3. Connect code in an `addOnLoad` function to call the `dojo.animateProperty` method when the `<div>` element is clicked.

4. Set the `start` and `end` values for the `height` and `width` properties to specify how the expansion should proceed.

5. Assign the `easing` property `function(t) {return t * t * t;}`.

6. Use the `play` method to execute the animation.

   Script 8.6 shows how your page should look after you make the additions.

Script 8.6 Expanding elements with easing functions.

```
1   <html>
2    <head>
3     <title>Expanding Elements with
4      Functions</title>
5
6     <link rel="stylesheet"
7      type="text/css" href=
8      "http://o.aolcdn.com/dojo/1.1/
9      dojo/resources/dojo.css" />
10
11    <link rel="stylesheet"
12     type="text/css"
13     href="http://o.aolcdn.com/
14     dojo/1.1/dijit/themes/
15     tundra/tundra.css" />
16
17    <style type="text/css">
18     .div {
19       width : 100px;
20       height : 100px;
21       background : cyan;
22     }
23    </style>
24
25    <script
26     type="text/javascript"
27     src="http://o.aolcdn.com/
28     dojo/1.1/dojo/dojo.xd.js">
29    </script>
30
31    <script type="text/javascript">
32     dojo.addOnLoad(function() {
33     var div = dojo.byId("div");
34     dojo.connect(div, "onclick",
35       function(evt) {
36     dojo.animateProperty({
37       node : div,
38       duration : 1000,
39       easing : function(t) {return t *
40         t * t;},
41       properties : {
42         height : {start : '100',
```

(script continues)

Script 8.6 *continued*

```
43            end : '200'},
44            width : {start : '100',
45            end : '200'}
46          }
47        }).play();
48      });
49    });
50    </script>
51  </head>
52
53  <body>
54    <h1>Expanding Elements with
55      Functions</h1>
56
57    <div id="div" class="div">
58      <h1>Click me</h1>
59      <input type="text"
60        value="hello"></input>
61    </div>
62  </body>
63  </html>
```

7. Save your file.

8. Navigate to your file in a browser.

9. Click the <div> element to make it expand. In this case, it will double its size in both dimensions slowly at first, and then faster, following the easing function (**Figure 8.6**).

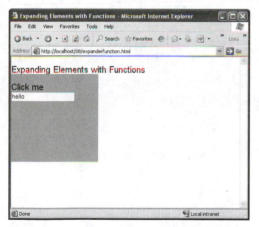

Figure 8.6 The <div> element after expansion using an easing function.

Animating Drag-and-Drop Operations

You can combine animation with drag-and-drop operations—for instance, to provide a visual guide for the user. To use an animation effect at the conclusion of a drag-and-drop operation, you just subscribe to the /dnd/move/stop event and execute your animation when that event occurs.

The example drag.html displays an image that you can drag; when you drop the image, it fades out.

To use animation with drag-and-drop operations:

1. Open your Web page in a text editor.

2. Create an <img> element with the ID "image" that's styled to set its absolute position to (100, 100) and displays the image you want to drag.

3. Connect code in an addOnLoad function to call the dojo.fadeOut method when the image's /dnd/move/stop event occurs.

4. Use the play method to execute the animation.

   Script 8.7 shows how your page should look after you make the additions.

Script 8.7 Using animation with drag-and-drop operations.

```
1    <html>
2      <head>
3        <title>Drag and Drop with
4          Animation</title>
5
6        <style>
7          .image {
8            position : absolute;
9            left : 100px;
10           top : 100px;
11         }
12       </style>
13
14       <script
15         type="text/javascript"
16         djConfig="parseOnLoad:true"
17         src="http://o.aolcdn.com/
18         dojo/1.1/dojo/dojo.xd.js">
19       </script>
20
21       <script type="text/javascript">
22         dojo.require("dojo.parser");
23         dojo.require("dojo.dnd.move");
24
25         dojo.addOnLoad(function(){
26           dojo.subscribe("/dnd/move/stop",
27           function(evt){
28            dojo.fadeOut({
29              node: evt.node,
30              duration:1000
31            }).play();
32           });
33         });
34       </script>
35
36     </head>
37
38     <body>
39
40       <h1>Drag and Drop with Animation</h1>
41
42       <img class="image" id="image"
43         dojoType="dojo.dnd.Moveable"
44         src="person.jpg"/>
45
46     </body>
47   </html>
```

Figure 8.7 A draggable image.

5. Save your file.

6. Navigate to your file in a browser. You should see the image (**Figure 8.7**).

7. Drag the image and then drop it. When you drop it, the image fades out.

ANIMATING DRAG-AND-DROP OPERATIONS

Toggling Elements Between Visible and Invisible

You can toggle elements from visible to invisible and back again with the `dojo.fx.Toggler` show and `hide` methods.

The example toggler.html displays a `<div>` element with some text and an HTML text field; the whole `<div>` element, with its enclosed text and text field, toggles between visible and invisible when you click it.

To toggle elements between visible and invisible:

1. Open your Web page in a text editor.

2. Add a `dojo.require("dojo.fx");` statement to your code.

3. Create a new `<div>` element styled to have a cyan background and enclosing some text and an HTML text field.

4. Connect code to the `<div>` element's `onclick` event to call the `dojo.fx.Toggler` show or `hide` method to show or hide the `<div>` element.

   Script 8.8 shows how your page should look after you make the additions.

Script 8.8 Toggling elements between visible and invisible.

```
1   <html>
2     <head>
3       <title>Toggling Elements</title>
4       <link rel="stylesheet"
5         type="text/css"
6         href="http://o.aolcdn.com/dojo/1.1/
7         dojo/resources/dojo.css" />
8
9       <link rel="stylesheet"
10        type="text/css"
11        href="http://o.aolcdn.com/
12        dojo/1.1/dijit/themes/
13        tundra/tundra.css" />
14
15      <style type="text/css">
16        .div {
17          width : 100px;
18          height : 100px;
19          background : cyan;
20        }
21      </style>
22
23      <script
24        type="text/javascript"
25        src="http://o.aolcdn.com/
26        dojo/1.1/dojo/dojo.xd.js">
27      </script>
28
29      <script type="text/javascript">
30        dojo.require("dojo.fx");
31
32        dojo.addOnLoad(function( ) {
33        var div = dojo.byId("div");
34        var toggler = new dojo.fx.Toggler({
35          node : div,
36          showDuration : 1000,
37          hideDuration : 1000
38        });
39        var seen = true;
40        dojo.connect(div, "onclick",
41          function(evt) {
42          seen = !seen;
43          if (seen)
44            toggler.show();
45          else
```

(script continues)

Script 8.8 *continued*

```
        script
46              toggler.hide();
47          });
48      });
49    </script>
50  </head>
51
52  <body>
53    <h1>Toggling Elements</h1>
54
55    <div id="div" class="div">
56      <h1>Click me</h1>
57      <input type="text"
58      value="hello"></input>
59    </div>
60
61  </body>
62 </html>
```

5. Save your file.

6. Navigate to your file in a browser. You should see the <div> element with an HTML text field (**Figure 8.8**).

7. Click the <div> element; it toggles to invisible. Click again where the element was; it becomes visible again.

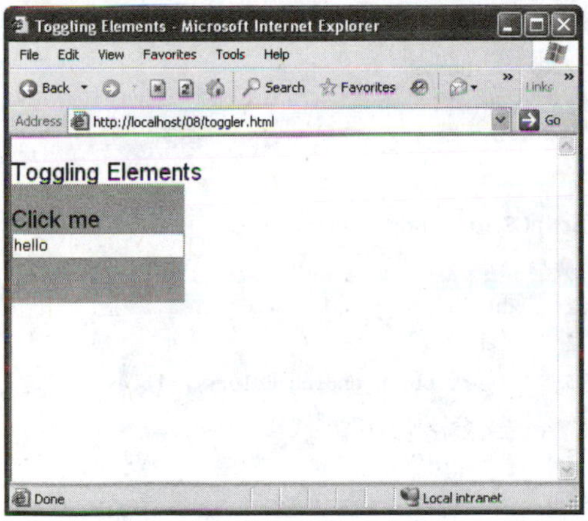

Figure 8.8 A <div> element that can be toggled.

Blending Colors

You can use the Dojo `blendColors` method to blend colors. You can display blended colors using this effect (the colors are blended off-screen, though; the blending does not appear as a visual operation).

The example blender.html blends yellow and red and displays the result.

To blend colors:

1. Open your Web page in a text editor.

2. Create a new `<div>` element of 100 x 100 pixels.

    Script 8.9 shows how your page should look after you make the additions.

3. Connect code to create the colors yellow and red using `dojo.Color`.

4. Use `dojo.blendColors` to blend the yellow and red colors, giving each a weight of 0.5 to mix the colors evenly.

5. Use `dojo.style` to style the `<div>` element with the blended color.

    Script 8.10 shows how your page should look after you make the additions.

Script 8.9 Creating a `<div>` element to blend colors.

```
1    <html>
2      <head>
3        <title>Blending Colors</title>
4        <style type="text/css">
5          .div {
6            width : 100px;
7            height : 100px;
8          }
9        </style>
10       <script type="text/javascript"
11         src="http://o.aolcdn.com/
12         dojo/1.1/dojo/dojo.xd.js">
13       </script>
14     </head>
15     <body>
16       <h1>Blending Colors</h1>
17       Yellow + Red =
18       <br>
19       <div id="div" class="div"></div>
20     </body>
21   </html>
```

Script 8.10 Blending colors.

```
1    <html>
2      <head>
3        <title>Blending Colors</title>
4        <style type="text/css">
5          .div {
6            width : 100px;
7            height : 100px;
8          }
9        </style>
10
11       <script type="text/javascript"
12         src="http://o.aolcdn.com/
13         dojo/1.1/dojo/dojo.xd.js">
14       </script>
15
16       <script type="text/javascript">
17         dojo=.addOnLoad(function() {
```

(script continues)

Script 8.10 *continued*

```
18        var yellow = new
19          dojo.Color("yellow");
20
21        var red = new dojo.Color(
22          [255, 0, 0]);
23
24        var blend =
25          dojo.blendColors(yellow, red,
26          0.5);
27
28        dojo.style("div", "background",
29          blend.toCss(  ));
30        });
31      </script>
32    </head>
33
34    <body>
35      <h1>Blending Colors</h1>
36      Yellow + Red =
37      <br>
38      <div id="div" class="div"></div>
39    </body>
40  </html>
```

6. Save your file.

7. Navigate to your file in a browser. You should see the `<div>` element displaying the blended color (**Figure 8.9**).

✔ Tip

- You can couple color-blending operations with a Dijit color picker to let the user select colors not displayed by the color picker when the user clicks the picker multiple times.

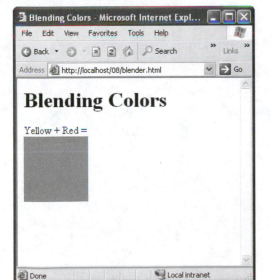

Figure 8.9 A blended color.

AJAX

Ajax is a big topic in the computing world—and it's a big topic in Dojo, too. Dojo is emerging as the premiere JavaScript library for Ajax.

Ajax allows browsers to fetch data from the server without a page refresh, so you don't get any of that flash and flicker so common in the browsing experience. Instead, Ajax-enabled Web pages look and feel much more like desktop applications: you click a button, and the data you want appears somewhere in the page. The whole page stays the same except for that data.

Using Ajax, for example, you can buy an item without the need for five or six page refreshes—you might just drag the item to a shopping cart icon, and behind the scenes Ajax would contact the server, get the price, display a checkout form in which you can enter your information, and send your completed form to the server.

Ajax sends and receives data to the Web server using an object built into modern Web browsers: the `XHMLHttpRequest` (XHR for short in Dojo) object.

You will need to place the examples in this chapter on a Web server. That wasn't necessary for the previous chapters, but here, the browser has to use the `XMLHttpRequest` object, and to do that, it needs to interact with an actual Web server.

Using Ajax Without Dojo

We'll start this chapter by looking at pre-Dojo Ajax, doing everything ourselves. Doing so will give you an idea of how much easier Dojo makes the process of applying Ajax to your Web pages. Here, you'll create an XMLHttpRequest object in a browser-dependent way, configure the XMLHttpRequest object, connect to the server, and download the data yourself.

This example ajax.html fetches the data in a text file, data.txt, from the server when a button is clicked and displays that data without refreshing the page.

✔ Tip

■ The term *Ajax* means asynchronous (that is, happening in the background) JavaScript and XML (XML is often used for the data).

To implement Ajax without Dojo:

1. Open your text editor and create a file named data.txt with the contents *Hello from Ajax*; store that file in a directory on a Web server.

2. Open your text editor and create ajax.html; store this file in the same directory as data.txt on the Web server.

3. Create an XMLHttpRequest object and configure it to use the GET method to fetch the data.txt file.

4. Connect an anonymous callback function to the XMLHttpRequest object's onreadystatechange property.

Script 9.1 Implementing Ajax without Dojo.

```
1   <html>
2    <head>
3     <title>An Ajax Example</title>
4     <script language = "javascript">
5       var XMLHttpRequestObject = false;
6       if (window.XMLHttpRequest) {
7         XMLHttpRequestObject = new
8         XMLHttpRequest();
9       } else if (window.ActiveXObject) {
10        XMLHttpRequestObject = new
11        ActiveXObject(
12        "Microsoft.XMLHTTP");}
13      function getData(dataSource, divID){
14        if(XMLHttpRequestObject) {
15          var obj = document
16          .getElementById(divID);
17          XMLHttpRequestObject
18          .open("GET", dataSource);
19          XMLHttpRequestObject
20          .onreadystatechange =function(){
21          if (XMLHttpRequestObject.
22          readyState == 4 &&
23          XMLHttpRequestObject.status ==
24          200) {
25            obj.innerHTML =
26            XMLHttpRequestObject
27            .responseText;
28          }
29          }
30          XMLHttpRequestObject
31          .send(null);
32        }
33      }
34     </script>
35   </head>
36   <body>
37     <h1>An Ajax Example</h1>
38     <form>
39       <input type = "button" value =
40       "Fetch the message"
41       onclick = "getData('data.txt',
42       'targetDiv')">
43     </form>
44     <div id="targetDiv">
45       <p>The fetched message will appear
46       here.</p>
47     </div>
48   </body>
49   </html>
```

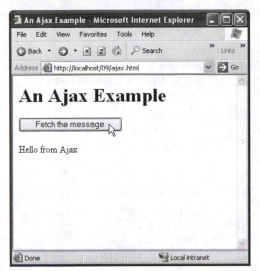

Figure 9.1 Downloading data using Ajax.

5. Wait until the XMLHttpRequest object's readyState property equals 4 and the status property equals 200; then display the downloaded data, getting it from the XMLHttpRequest object's responseText property.

Script 9.1 shows how your page should look after you make the additions.

6. Save ajax.html.

7. Navigate to ajax.html in a browser and click the button. The ajax.html page uses Ajax to download data.txt without a screen refresh and display its contents in the Web page (**Figure 9.1**).

✔ Tip

■ Although the process is lengthy, it's worth knowing how to implement Ajax on your own to perform advanced tasks that Dojo can't.

Using the Dojo xhrGet Method

Dojo makes using Ajax far simpler than the process you saw in the first task in this chapter. You can use Ajax to read data from the server using either the GET or POST HTTP request method; here, you'll see how to use the Dojo xhrGet method to implement a GET operation.

The example ajaxget.html uses xhrGet to get the same data.txt file as the example in the previous task, but this time, you'll implement Ajax the Dojo way. This example downloads and displays the contents of data.txt as soon as the page opens in the browser.

You pass various named parameters to the xhrGet method: url holds the URL of the data you want to fetch, load holds a function to be called back with the response from the server (that is, the downloaded data), and handleAs indicates that in this example you want to handle the downloaded data as text.

To use Ajax with Dojo:

1. Open your text editor and create a file named data.txt with the contents *Hello from Ajax*; store that file in a directory on a Web server.

2. Open your text editor and create ajaxget. html; store this file in the same directory as data.txt on the Web server.

3. Call dojo.xhrGet, and with the url para-meter specify the URL of the data to down-load ("data.txt"), with the handleAs parameter specify the data format as "text", and with the load parameter specify the anonymous function to call to display the downloaded data in the Web page.

Script 9.2 Using Ajax with Dojo.

```
1   <html>
2    <head>
3     <title>Using Ajax Get</title>
4
5     <script
6       type="text/javascript"
7       src="http://o.aolcdn.com/
8       dojo/1.1/dojo/dojo.xd.js">
9     </script>
10    <script type="text/javascript">
11     dojo.addOnLoad(function() {
12     dojo.xhrGet({
13       url : "data.txt",
14       handleAs : "text",
15       load : function(response, args)
16       {
17         dojo.byId("div").innerHTML =
18           response;
19         return response;
20       }
21     });
22     });
23    </script>
24   </head>
25
26   <body>
27     <h1>Using Ajax Get</h1>
28     <br>
29     <div id="div"></div>
30   </body>
31  </html>
```

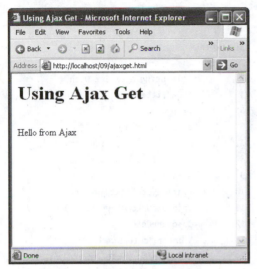

Figure 9.2 Using xhrGet to download data.

4. Add code to the anonymous function to handle the downloaded text passed in the `response` parameter by displaying that text in a `<div>` element in the Web page. Make sure you return the `response` parameter from the anonymous function.

Script 9.2 shows how your page should look after you make the additions.

5. Save ajaxget.html.

6. Navigate to ajaxget.html in a browser. This example downloads and displays the data in data.txt (**Figure 9.2**).

✔ Tips

■ Notice how much simpler it was to use Dojo's `xhrGet` method than to write all the Ajax code yourself as you did in the previous task.

■ We downloaded a static text file here, but of course you can read text returned by an online program, such as a PHP file. Examples are coming up in this chapter.

Using Dojo xhrGet to Read XML

The previous task showed how to get text from a Web server using Dojo's xhrGet method—but Ajax means asynchronous JavaScript with XML, so now we'll look at how to download XML.

The main difference with XML is that the response from the server is passed to your code as a JavaScript XML object, and that process takes a little getting used to.

The example ajaxxml.html downloads colors.xml, a list of colors in XML format, and displays the list.

To download XML with Ajax:

1. Open your text editor and create a file named colors.xml; store that file in a directory on a Web server and give it this content:

```
<?xml version = "1.0" ?>
<colors>
  <color>red</color>
  <color>green</color>
  <color>blue</color>
</colors>
```

2. Open your text editor and create ajaxgetxml.html. Store the file in the same directory as colors.xml on the Web server.

3. Call dojo.xhrGet, and with the url parameter specify the URL of the data you want to download ("colors.xml"), with the handleAs parameter specify the data format as "xml", and with the load parameter specify the anonymous function to call to display the downloaded data in the Web page.

Script 9.3 Downloading XML with Ajax.

```
1   <html>
2    <head>
3     <title>Using Ajax Get with
4      XML</title>
5     <script
6      type="text/javascript"
7      src="http://o.aolcdn.com/
8      dojo/1.1/dojo/dojo.xd.js">
9     </script>
10    <script type="text/javascript">
11     dojo.addOnLoad(function() {
12      dojo.xhrGet({
13       url : "colors.xml",
14       handleAs : "xml",
15       load : function(response, args)
16        var obj = document
17         .getElementById("color");
18        colors = response
19         .getElementsByTagName("color");
20        obj.innerHTML = "Here are the
21         fetched colors:<ul>";
22        for (loopIndex = 0; loopIndex <
23        colors.length; loopIndex++ )
24        {
25         obj.innerHTML += "<li>" +
26         colors[loopIndex]
27          .firstChild.data + "</li>";
28        }
29        obj.innerHTML += "</ul>";
30        return response;
31       }
32      });
33     });
34    </script>
35   </head>
36   <body>
37    <h1>Using Ajax Get with XML</h1>
38    <br>
39    <div name="color" id="color"></div>
40   </body>
41  </html>
```

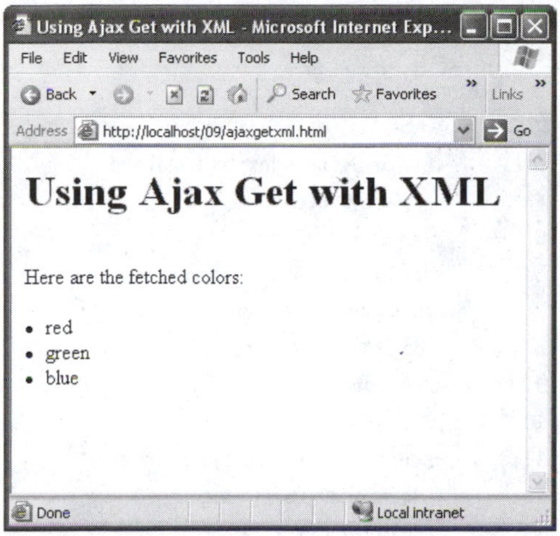

Figure 9.3 The list of colors from colors.xml.

4. Add code to the anonymous function to handle the downloaded XML object passed in the `response` parameter by calling the `getElementsByTagName` method to extract the `<color>` elements and using the `firstChild.data` property to access the text inside each `<color>` element, displaying that text in a `<div>` element in the Web page.

Script 9.3 shows how your page should look after you make the additions.

5. Save ajaxgetxml.html.

6. Navigate to ajaxgetxml.html in a browser. You should see the colors from colors.xml listed, fetched using Ajax (**Figure 9.3**).

Using Dojo xhrGet to Read JSON

You can use the `dojo.xhrGet` method to download data in JavaScript Object Notation—or JSON—format.

The example ajagetjson.html downloads a JSON file. In code, you can refer to the fields in the JSON data as properties of the response object passed to your anonymous download function.

To fetch JSON data using Ajax:

1. Open your text editor and create a file named data.json; store that file in a directory on a Web server and give it this content:

   ```
   {
     "key1" : 1234,
     "key2" : 2345,
     "key3" : 3456,
     "key3" : 4567
   }
   ```

2. Open your text editor and create ajaxgetjson.html; store this file in the same directory as data.json on the Web server.

3. Call `dojo.xhrGet`, and with the `url` parameter specify the URL of the data you want to download (`"data.json"`), with the `handleAs` parameter specify the data format as `"json"`, and with the `load` parameter specify the anonymous function to call to display the downloaded data in the Web page.

Script 9.4 Fetching JSON data with Ajax.

```
1   <html>
2     <head>
3       <title>Using Ajax to Download
4       JSON</title>
5
6       <script type="text/javascript"
7         src="http://o.aolcdn.com/
8         dojo/1.1/dojo/dojo.xd.js">
9       </script>
10
11      <script type="text/javascript">
12        dojo.addOnLoad(function() {
13        dojo.xhrGet({
14          url : "data.json",
15          handleAs : "json",
16          load : function(response, args) {
17          dojo.byId("div").innerHTML=
18          "The value for key 2 is " +
19          response.key2;
20
21          return response;
22        }
23        });
24        });
25      </script>
26
27    </head>
28
29    <body>
30      <h1>Using Ajax to Download JSON</h1>
31      <br>
32
33      <div id="div"></div>
34
35    </body>
36  </html>
```

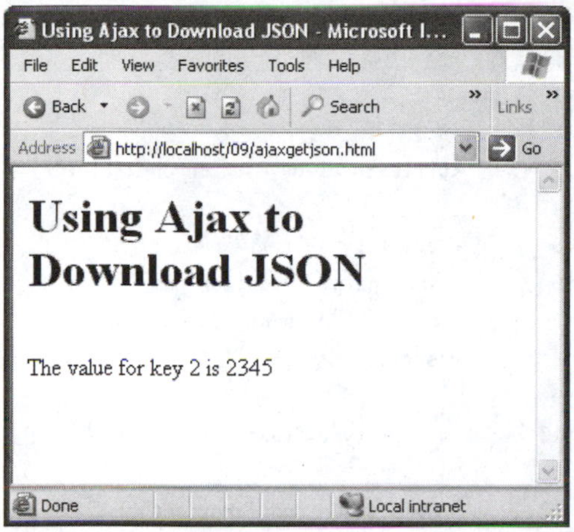

Figure 9.4 The value for the key2 field.

4. Add code to the anonymous function to handle the downloaded JSON object passed in the `response` parameter by accessing the value connected with the key2 field and then display that value in the Web page.

   Script 9.4 shows how your page should look after you make the additions.

5. Save ajaxgetjson.html.

6. Navigate to ajaxgetjson.html in a browser. You should see the value connected to the key2 field, fetched using Ajax (**Figure 9.4**).

Handling Dojo xhrGet Errors

Sometimes, Ajax operations lead to errors, as when the file or URL you're trying to access is missing. You can set up the Dojo xhrGet method to handle errors.

The example ajaxgeterror.html tries to fetch a nonexistent file, data2.txt, from the server. When the Ajax operation to fetch the file fails, an error message appears.

To handle xhrGet errors:

1. Open your text editor and create ajaxgeterror.html; store it in the same directory as data.txt on the Web server.

2. Call dojo.xhrGet, and with the url parameter specify the URL of the data you want to download (in this case, the nonexistent file "data2.txt"), with the handleAs parameter specify the data format as "text", and with the load parameter specify the anonymous function to call to display the downloaded data in the Web page.

3. Add code to the anonymous function to handle the downloaded text passed in the response parameter by displaying that text in a <div> element in the Web page. Make sure you return the response parameter from the anonymous function.

4. Add a function to display an error message under the error parameter in the xhrGet method call. Make that function display an error message in the Web page.

   Script 9.5 shows how your page should look after you make the additions.

```
1   <html>
2     <head>
3       <title>Handling Ajax Errors</title>
4
5       <script type="text/javascript"
6         src="http://o.aolcdn.com/
7         dojo/1.1/dojo/dojo.xd.js">
8       </script>
9
10      <script type="text/javascript">
11
12        dojo.addOnLoad(function() {
13
14          dojo.xhrGet({
15            url : "data2.txt",
16            handleAs : "text",
17            load : function(response, args) {
18              dojo.byId("div").innerHTML=
19                response;
20              return response;
21            },
22            error : function(response, args){
23              dojo.byId("div").innerHTML=
24                "Error fetching data2.txt!";
25              return response;
26            }
27
28          });
29        });
30      </script>
31
32    </head>
33
34    <body>
35      <h1>Handling Ajax Errors</h1>
36      <br>
37
38      <div id="div">
39      </div>
40
41    </body>
42  </html>
```

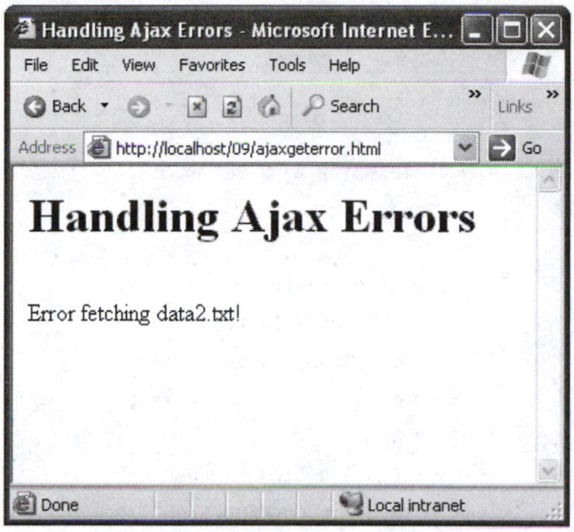

Figure 9.5 A message indicating an Ajax error.

5. Save ajaxgeterror.html.

6. Navigate to ajaxgeterror.html in a browser. You should see an error message as the process tries to download the nonexistent file data2.txt (**Figure 9.5**).

✔ Tip

- You can specify a timeout value in milliseconds with the `timeout` parameter. If the Ajax operation doesn't complete before the specified time elapses, your error handler will be called.

Sending Data Using GET

Usually when you use Ajax, you send data to the server to customize the data you get back. You'll see how to do this in this task.

The example ajaxgetdata.html sends data to a script on the server, dataresponder.php, that reads what you sent as the parameter named data and sends back a text string depending on whether you sent a value of 1 or 2; then the Ajax Web page displays that message.

✔ Tip

■ You need to place the files in this example on a Web server that runs PHP.

To send Ajax data using GET:

1. Open your text editor and create a file named dataresponder.php; store that file in a directory on a Web server and give it this content:

```php
<?php
  if ($_GET["data"] == "1") {
    echo 'The server got a value of
    → 1';
  }
  if ($_GET["data"] == "2") {
    echo 'The server got a value of
    → 2';
  }
?>
```

2. Open your text editor and create ajaxgetdata.html; store this file in the same directory as dataresponder.php on the Web server.

Script 9.6 Sending Ajax data using GET.

```
1    <html>
2      <head>
3        <title>Using Ajax Get with
4          Data</title>
5
6        <script type="text/javascript"
7          src="http://o.aolcdn.com/
8          dojo/1.1/dojo/dojo.xd.js">
9        </script>
10
11       <script type="text/javascript">
12         dojo.addOnLoad(function() {
13           dojo.xhrGet({
14             url : "dataresponder.php",
15
16             handleAs : "text",
17
18             content: {data : '1'},
19
20             load: function(response,args) {
21               dojo.byId("div").innerHTML=
22               response;
23
24               return response;
25             },
26
27             error:function(response,args) {
28               dojo.byId("div").innerHTML=
29               "Error";
30               return response;
31             }
32
33           });
34         });
35       </script>
36     </head>
37
38     <body>
39       <h1>Using Ajax Get with Data</h1>
40       <br>
41       <div id="div"></div>
42     </body>
43   </html>
```

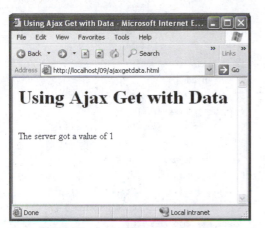

Figure 9.6 Sending and getting data using Ajax.

3. Call `dojo.xhrGet`, and with the `url` parameter specify the URL of the PHP file (`"dataresponder.php"`), with the `handleAs` parameter specify the data format as `"text"`, set the `content` parameter to `{data : '1'}` to send a 1 under the parameter named `"data"` to the server, and with the `load` parameter specify the anonymous function to call to display the downloaded data in the Web page.

4. Add code to the anonymous function to display the response from the server in the Web page.

   Script 9.6 shows how your page should look after you make the additions.

5. Save ajaxgetdata.html.

6. Navigate to ajaxgetdata.html in a browser. You should see the text "The server got a value of 1" because the example sent a 1 to the server and received the correct response (**Figure 9.6**).

Using GET with Forms

Sometimes you may collect data using HTML forms that you want to send to the server. Dojo has a shortcut for sending all the data in a form to the server: you use the xhrGet method's form parameter.

The example ajaxgetform.html displays a form with a text box containing the ID "data". This example places an exclamation point (!) in the text box and then sends the form's data to the dataresponder.php script on the server (see the previous task for information about dataresponder.php). That PHP script returns a text string indicating whether you sent a 1 or a 2 to it, and this example then displays that text string.

To send form data using an Ajax GET operation:

1. Open your text editor and create a file named dataresponder.php; store that file in a directory on a Web server and give it this content:

```php
<?php
  if ($_GET["data"] == "1") {
    echo 'The server got a value of
    → 1';
  }
  if ($_GET["data"] == "2") {
    echo 'The server got a value of
    → 2';
  }
?>
```

2. Open your text editor and create ajaxgetform.html; store this file in the same directory as dataresponder.php on the Web server.

Script 9.7 Sending form data using an Ajax GET operation.

```
1    <html>
2      <head>
3        <title>Using Ajax Get with
4          Forms</title>
5        <script type="text/javascript"
6          src="http://o.aolcdn.com/
7          dojo/1.1/dojo/dojo.xd.js">
8        </script>
9        <script type="text/javascript">
10         dojo.addOnLoad(function() {
11         dojo.xhrGet({
12           url : "dataresponder.php",
13           handleAs : "text",
14           form : dojo.byId("form"),
15           load : function(response, args) {
16             dojo.byId("div").innerHTML=
17               response;
18             return response;
19           },
20           error: function(response, args) {
21             dojo.byId("div").innerHTML=
22             "Error";
23             return response;
24           }
25         });
26         });
27       </script>
28     </head>
29     <body>
30       <h1>Using Ajax Get with Forms</h1>
31       <br>
32       <form
33         dojoType="dijit.form.Form"
34         id="form">
35         Enter 1 or 2:
36         <input dojoType=
37         "dijit.form.TextBox"
38         name="data" id="data"
39         value="1"></input>
40       </form>
41       <div id="div"></div>
42     </body>
43   </html>
```

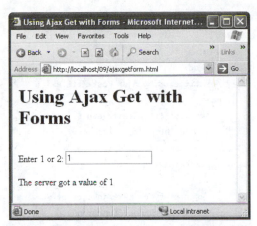

Figure 9.7 Sending and getting form data using Ajax.

3. Call dojo.xhrGet, and with the url parameter specify the URL of the PHP file ("dataresponder.php"), with the handleAs parameter specify the data format as "text", set the form parameter to dojo.byId("form") (where "form" is the ID of the form), and with the load parameter specify the anonymous function to call to display the downloaded data in the Web page.

4. Add a <form> element containing a text box and the ID "data" containing the value "1".

5. Add code to the anonymous function to display the response from the server in the Web page.

Script 9.7 shows how your page should look after you make the additions.

6. Save ajaxgetform.html.

7. Navigate to ajaxgetform.html in a browser. You should see the text "The server got a value of 1" because the example sent the 1 in the text box to the server and received the correct response (**Figure 9.7**).

Sending Data Using POST

In addition to the GET HTTP method, you can use the POST method. The POST method is somewhat more secure than the GET method: whereas GET appends any data sent to the server to the URL it accesses, POST encodes that data in HTTP headers, making it less accessible to prying eyes.

The example ajaxpostdata.html sends data to a script on the server, dataresponderpost. php, that reads what you posted as the parameter named *data* and sends back a text string depending on whether you sent a value of 1 or 2; then the Ajax Web page displays that message.

✔ Tip

■ You need to place the files in this example on a Web server that runs PHP.

To send Ajax data using POST:

1. Open your text editor and create a file named dataresponderpost.php; store that file in a directory on a Web server and give it this content:

```php
<?php
  if ($_POST["data"] == "1") {
    echo 'The server got a value of
    → 1';
  }
  if ($_POST["data"] == "2") {
    echo 'The server got a value of
    → 2';
  }
?>
```

2. Open your text editor and create ajax-postdata.html; store this file in the same directory as dataresponderpost.php on the Web server.

Script 9.8 Sending Ajax data using POST.

```
1   <html>
2     <head>
3       <title>Using Ajax Post</title>
4
5       <script type="text/javascript"
6         src="http://o.aolcdn.com/
7         dojo/1.1/dojo/dojo.xd.js">
8       </script>
9
10      <script type="text/javascript">
11        dojo.addOnLoad(function() {
12        dojo.xhrPost({
13          url : "dataresponderpost.php",
14          handleAs : "text",
15          content: {data : '1'},
16          load : function(response, args) {
17            dojo.byId("div").innerHTML=
18            response;
19            return response;
20          },
21          error : function(response, args)
22            dojo.byId("div").innerHTML=
23            "Error";
24            return response;
25          }
26        });
27        });
28      </script>
29    </head>
30
31    <body>
32      <h1>Using Ajax Post</h1>
33      <br>
34      <div id="div"></div>
35    </body>
36  </html>
```

Figure 9.8 Sending and getting data using POST and Ajax.

3. Call `dojo.xhrPost`, and with the `url` parameter specify the URL of the PHP file (`"dataresponder.php"`), with the `handleAs` parameter specify the data format as `"text"`, set the `content` parameter to `{data : '1'}` to send a 1 under the parameter named `"data"` to the server, and with the `load` parameter specify the anonymous function to call to display the downloaded data in the Web page.

4. Add code to the anonymous function to display the response from the server in the Web page.

Script 9.8 shows how your page should look after you make the additions.

5. Save ajaxpostdata.html.

6. Navigate to ajaxpostdata.html in a browser. You should see the text "The server got a value of 1" because the example sent a 1 to the server and received the correct response (**Figure 9.8**).

Advanced Ajax

We got started with Ajax in the previous chapter, but for a lot of people, Ajax is the main reason they turn to Dojo, so we'll delve into this topic further here.

In this chapter, you'll learn more about handling the errors that can crop up when you work with Ajax. You'll also learn how to chain callback functions (which are called when your downloaded data is ready), avoid having your browser cache a Web page whose data you're trying to download and whose data has changed (when a browser caches a Web page, it gives you the same version of the Web page no matter how many times you ask—and that's a serious problem in Ajax), handle Ajax timeouts, and more.

In other words, when you finish this chapter, you'll be an Ajax expert when it comes to Dojo.

As in the previous chapter, you will need to place the examples in this chapter on a Web server. That wasn't necessary for the chapters before Chapter 9, but here, the browser has to use the `XMLHttpRequest` object, and to do that, it needs to interact with an actual Web server.

Handling Ajax Timeouts

Ajax operations are asynchronous—that is, they don't stop the browser from doing other things while you're downloading data behind the scenes.

But Ajax operations also depend on the Internet, and that can be notoriously error prone. The file or script you're trying to access may not be there, there might be no Internet connection, the connection may be very slow, and so on. To avoid having the Ajax operation go on forever if a file you're trying to download isn't actually present, you should provide an Ajax timeout.

You do that with the `timeout` parameter of the `xhrGet` and `xhrPost` methods, setting that parameter to the number of milliseconds you want to wait before the operation is stopped.

The example ajaxtimeout.html tries to read a nonexistent file; the operation will time out after 1000 milliseconds (1 second), and an error handler will be called.

To set an Ajax timeout:

1. Open your text editor and create ajaxtimeout.html.

2. Call `dojo.xhrGet`, and with the `url` parameter specify the URL of the data you want to download (the nonexistent file "`data2.txt`"), with the `handleAs` parameter specify the data format as "`text`", and with the `load` parameter specify the anonymous function to call to display the downloaded data in the Web page. Set the `error` parameter to an error-handling function that displays the message "Ajax error!" and set the `timeout` parameter to 1000.

Script 10.1 Setting an Ajax timeout.

```
1   <html>
2     <head>
3       <title>Handling Ajax Timeouts</title>
4
5       <script type="text/javascript"
6         src="http://o.aolcdn.com/
7         dojo/1.1/dojo/dojo.xd.js">
8       </script>
9
10      <script type="text/javascript">
11        dojo.addOnLoad(function() {
12        dojo.xhrGet({
13          url : "data2.txt",
14
15          handleAs : "text",
16
17          timeout: 1000,
18
19          load : function(response, args) {
20            dojo.byId("div").innerHTML =
21              response;
22
23            return response;
24          },
25
26          error : function(response, args)
27          {
28            dojo.byId("div").innerHTML =
29              "Ajax error!";
30
31            return response;
32          }
33        });
34        });
35      </script>
36    </head>
37
38    <body>
39      <h1>Handling Ajax Timeouts</h1>
40      <br>
41
42      <div id="div"></div>
43    </body>
44  </html>
```

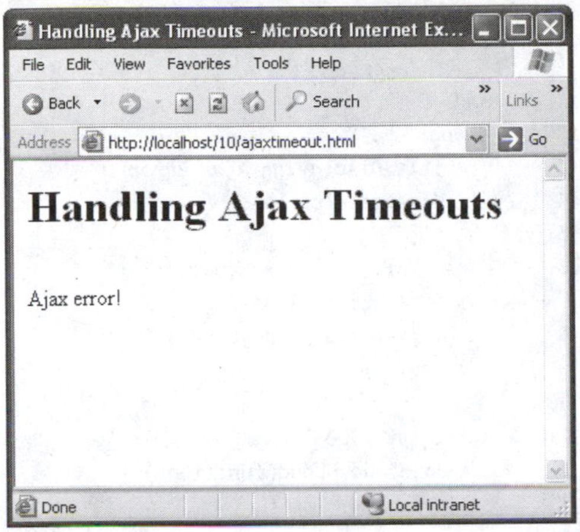

Figure 10.1 An Ajax timeout.

3. Add code to the anonymous function to handle the downloaded text passed in the `response` parameter by displaying that text in a `<div>` element in the Web page. Make sure you return the `response` parameter from the anonymous function.

Script 10.1 shows how your page should look after you make the additions.

4. Save ajaxtimeout.html.

5. Navigate to ajaxtimeout.html in a browser. This example attempts to download the nonexistent file in data2.txt and display it. When that file can't be found, the operation will time out (**Figure 10.1**).

Getting Error Messages

The previous example simply displayed the error message "Ajax error!" without saying what kind of error occurred. In fact, you don't know what the error actually was. Is there a way to find out?

Yes indeed. If an error occurs, you can display the message property of the response object, which holds a detailed error message.

The example ajaxerrorhandler.html attempts to download data from the URL http://www.fidhdnfgskre.com (this is probably the last domain name not taken on the Internet), and when the operations fails, it displays an error message explaining just what the problem is.

To display error messages:

1. Open your text editor and create ajaxerrorhandler.html.

2. Call dojo.xhrGet, and with the url parameter specify the URL of the data you want to download (the nonexistent domain "http://www.fidhdnfgskre.com"), with the handleAs parameter specify the data format as "text", and with the load parameter specify the anonymous function to call to display the downloaded data in the Web page. Set the error parameter to an error-handling function.

3. Add code to the anonymous function to handle errors by displaying response.message in a <div> element in the Web page. Make sure you return the response parameter from the anonymous function.

   Script 10.2 shows how your page should look after you make the additions.

Script 10.2 Displaying error messages.

```
1   <html>
2     <head>
3       <title>Displaying Ajax Error
4         Messages</title>
5
6       <script type="text/javascript"
7         src="http://o.aolcdn.com/
8         dojo/1.1/dojo/dojo.xd.js">
9       </script>
10
11      <script type="text/javascript">
12        dojo.addOnLoad(function() {
13          dojo.xhrGet({
14
15            url : "http://www.
16              fidhdnfgskre.com",
17
18            handleAs : "text",
19
20            timeOut: 100,
21
22            load : function(response, args) {
23
24              dojo.byId("div").innerHTML =
25                response;
26
27              return response;
28            },
29            error : function(response, args)
30            {
31
32              dojo.byId("div").innerHTML =
33                response.message;
34
35              return response;
36            }
37          });
38        });
39      </script>
40    </head>
41
42    <body>
43      <h1>Displaying Ajax Error
44        Messages</h1>
45      <br>
46      <div id="div"></div>
47    </body>
48  </html>
```

Figure 10.2 An Ajax error message.

4. Save ajaxerrorhandler.html.

5. Navigate to ajaxerrorhandler.html in a browser. This example attempts to go to the nonexistent URL http://www.fidhdnfgskre.com and display the page. When it can't find that URL, it displays a detailed error message: "Unable to load http://www.fidhdnfgskre.com status:0" (**Figure 10.2**).

Finishing Ajax Operations

You may need to perform some tasks regardless of whether an Ajax operation is successful: for instance, you may need to shut down an online database. But as you've seen, successful Ajax operations are handled by the function pointed to by the `load` parameter, and failed Ajax operations are handled by the function pointed to by the `error` parameter. How do you execute the same code whether or not an error occurs?

You can add finishing-up code to a function pointed to by the `handle` parameter. The code in that function runs regardless of whether an error occurs, giving you the perfect place to add to your application cleanup code that you want to run after the Ajax operation ends.

The example ajaxhandle.html attempts to read a nonexistent file, data2.txt and then displays an error message; then it runs some cleanup code (which would also have run if the Ajax operation had been successful) displaying a message about shutting down an online database.

To finish Ajax operations:

1. Open your text editor and create ajaxhandle.html.

2. Call `dojo.xhrGet`, and with the `url` parameter specify the URL of the data to download (the nonexistent file `"data2. txt"`) and with the `load` parameter specify the anonymous function to call to display the downloaded data in the Web page. Set the `error` parameter to an error-handling function that displays `response. message` and set the `handle` parameter to a function that displays a message about shutting down the database.

   Script 10.3 shows how your page should look after you make the additions.

Script 10.3 Finishing Ajax operations.

```
1   <html>
2     <head>
3       <title>Finishing Ajax
4         Operations</title>
5
6       <script type="text/javascript"
7         src="http://o.aolcdn.com/
8         dojo/1.1/dojo/dojo.xd.js">
9       </script>
10      <script type="text/javascript">
11      dojo.addOnLoad(function() {
12      dojo.xhrGet({
13        url : "data2.txt",
14        handleAs : "text",
15        timeOut: 1000,
16        load : function(response, args) {
17          dojo.byId("div").innerHTML =
18            response;
19          return response;
20        },
21        error : function(response, args)
22        {
23          dojo.byId("div").innerHTML =
24            response.message;
25          return response;
26        },
27        handle : function(response, args)
28        {
29          dojo.byId("div2").innerHTML =
30            "Shutting down database.";
31          return response;
32        }
33      });
34    });
35      </script>
36    </head>
37
38    <body>
39      <h1>Finishing Ajax Operations</h1>
40      <div id="div"></div>
41      <br>
42      <div id="div2"></div>
43    </body>
44  </html>
```

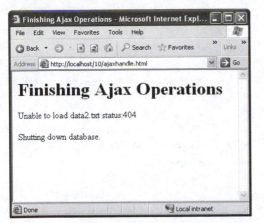

Figure 10.3 Finishing Ajax operations.

3. Save ajaxhandle.html.

4. Navigate to ajaxhandle.html in a browser. This example displays both an error message and a shutting-down message (**Figure 10.3**).

✔ Tip

- You can handle both successful and failed Ajax operations with just one function, pointed to by the `handle` parameter (without needing functions pointed to by the `load` and `error` parameters), and you can use the `if` statement `if (response instanceof Error){...}` to determine whether an error occurred.

Preventing Caching

Browser caching is a big problem in Ajax, especially with Internet Explorer. Suppose you request a page of data using Ajax behind the scenes, and the browser has already downloaded that page during the same browser session (the time from when the first browser window opens to when the last browser window closes). Even though the data in that page may have changed, the browser will give you cached data—that is, the Web page as it was when the browser downloaded it earlier.

Browser caching is a problem when you use xhrGet (but not xhrPost), but you can get around it by setting the preventCache parameter to true. Doing so causes Dojo to append a timestamp (as an ignored parameter) to the end of the URL you're accessing, making the URL you're accessing unique, so the browser can't cache it. So if you're getting stale data from an Ajax operation, set the preventCache parameter to true.

The example ajaxnocache.html demonstrates how to turn off browser caching.

To turn off browser caching:

1. Open your text editor and create a file named data.txt with the contents *Hello from Ajax*; store that file in a directory on a Web server.

2. Open your text editor and create ajaxnocache.html; store this file in the same directory as data.txt on the Web server.

Script 10.4 Turning off browser caching.

```
1   <html>
2     <head>
3       <title>Avoiding Browser Caching</title>
4
5       <script type="text/javascript"
6         src="http://o.aolcdn.com/
7         dojo/1.1/dojo/dojo.xd.js">
8       </script>
9
10      <script type="text/javascript">
11        dojo.addOnLoad(function() {
12        dojo.xhrGet({
13          url : "data.txt",
14          handleAs : "text",
15          timeout: 1000,
16          preventCache: true,
17          load : function(response, args) {
18            dojo.byId("div").innerHTML =
19            response;
20            return response;
21          },
22          error : function(response, args)
23          {
24            dojo.byId("div").innerHTML =
25            "Ajax error!";
26            return response;
27          }
28        });
29        });
30      </script>
31    </head>
32
33    <body>
34      <h1>Avoiding Browser Caching</h1>
35      <br>
36      <div id="div"></div>
37    </body>
38  </html>
```

Figure 10.4 Using xhrGet to download data without browser caching.

3. Call `dojo.xhrGet`, and with the `url` parameter specify the URL of the data you want to download (`"data.txt"`), with the `handleAs` parameter specify the data format as `"text"`, with the `load` parameter specify the anonymous function to call to display the downloaded data in the Web page, and set the `preventCache` parameter to `true`.

4. Add code to the anonymous function to handle the downloaded text passed in the `response` parameter by displaying that text in a `<div>` element in the Web page. Make sure you return the `response` parameter from the anonymous function.

Script 10.4 shows how your page should look after you make the additions.

5. Save ajaxnocache.html.

6. Navigate to ajaxnocache.html in a browser. This example downloads and displays the data in data.txt without browser caching (**Figure 10.4**).

Making Ajax Operations Synchronous

Ajax operates asynchronously—that is, it downloads and uploads its data behind the scenes without making the browser wait until it's done. However, sometimes you may need Ajax operations to take place synchronously—you may need the browser to wait until crucial data is downloaded before making use of that data and proceeding. For example, you may need a database record to download before the user can proceed. In such cases, you may want to make Ajax work synchronously—that is, you may want to block the browser from doing anything else until the download or upload is complete.

The example ajaxsync.html downloads a file synchronously, making the browser wait for the file to be downloaded before doing anything else. You make an Ajax operation synchronous by setting the sync parameter to true.

To make Ajax operations synchronous:

1. Open your text editor and create a file named data.txt with the contents *Hello from Ajax*; store that file in a directory on a Web server.

2. Open your text editor and create ajaxsync.html; store this file in the same directory as data.txt on the Web server.

3. Call dojo.xhrGet, and with the url parameter specify the URL of the data you want to download ("data.txt"), with the handleAs parameter specify the data format as "text", with the load parameter specify the anonymous function to call to display the downloaded data in the Web page, and set the sync parameter to true to make the operation synchronous.

Script 10.5 Making Ajax operations synchronous.

```
1   <html>
2    <head>
3     <title>Making Ajax
4      Synchronous</title>
5
6     <script type="text/javascript"
7       src="http://o.aolcdn.com/
8       dojo/1.1/dojo/dojo.xd.js">
9     </script>
10
11    <script type="text/javascript">
12     dojo.addOnLoad(function() {
13      dojo.xhrGet({
14       url : "data.txt",
15       handleAs : "text",
16       timeOut: 1000,
17       preventCase: true,
18       sync : true,
19       load : function(response, args) {
20        dojo.byId("div").innerHTML =
21         response;
22        return response;
23       },
24       error : function(response, args)
25       {
26        dojo.byId("div").innerHTML =
27         "Ajax error!";
28        return response;
29       }
30      });
31     });
32    </script>
33   </head>
34
35   <body>
36    <h1>Making Ajax Synchronous</h1>
37    <br>
38    <div id="div"></div>
39   </body>
40  </html>
```

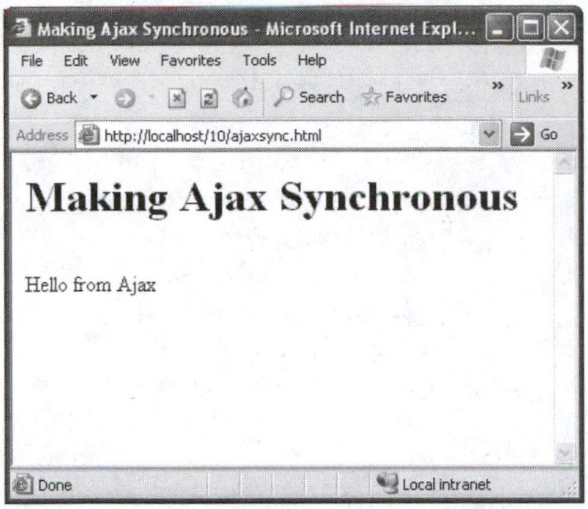

Figure 10.5 Making the browser wait until data is downloaded.

4. Add code to the anonymous function to handle the downloaded text passed in the `response` parameter by displaying that text in a `<div>` element in the Web page. Make sure you return the `response` parameter from the anonymous function.

Script 10.5 shows how your page should look after you make the additions.

5. Save ajaxsync.html.

6. Navigate to ajaxsync.html in a browser. This example synchronously downloads and displays the data in data.txt (**Figure 10.5**).

Getting the XMLHttpRequest Object

Dojo gives you direct access to the XMLHttpRequest object that is the heart of Ajax. That's good if you're a hotshot Ajax programmer and want to configure or use the XMLHttpRequest object in some advanced way.

To access the XMLHttpRequest object directly, you refer to the xhr property of the args parameter passed to your Ajax callback function.

The example ajaxdirect.html uses the XMLHttpRequest object's responseText property to access the text that was downloaded by the Ajax operation.

To access the XMLHttpRequest object directly:

1. Open your text editor and create a file named data.txt with the contents *Hello from Ajax*; store that file in a directory on a Web server.

2. Open your text editor and create ajaxdirect.html; store this file in the same directory as data.txt on the Web server.

3. Call dojo.xhrGet, and with the url parameter specify the URL of the data you want to download ("data.txt"), with the handleAs parameter specify the data format as "text", and with the load parameter specify the anonymous function to call to display the downloaded data in the Web page.

4. Add code to the anonymous function to display the xhr property's responseText property in the Web page.

   Script 10.6 shows how your page should look after you make the additions.

Script 10.6 Accessing the XMLHttpRequest object directly.

```
1   <html>
2    <head>
3     <title>Using the XMLHttpRequest
4       Object Directly</title>
5
6     <script type="text/javascript"
7       src="http://o.aolcdn.com/
8       dojo/1.1/dojo/dojo.xd.js">
9     </script>
10
11    <script type="text/javascript">
12     dojo.addOnLoad(function() {
13      dojo.xhrGet({
14
15       url : "data.txt",
16
17       handleAs : "text",
18
19       load : function(response, args) {
20
21        dojo.byId("div").innerHTML=
22         args.xhr.responseText;
23
24        return response;
25       },
26       error : function(response, args)
27       {
28        dojo.byId("div").innerHTML =
29         "Ajax error";
30
31        return response;
32       }
33      });
34     });
35    </script>
36   </head>
37
38   <body>
39    <h1>Using the XMLHttpRequest Object
40      Directly</h1>
41    <br>
42    <div id="div"></div>
43   </body>
44  </html>
```

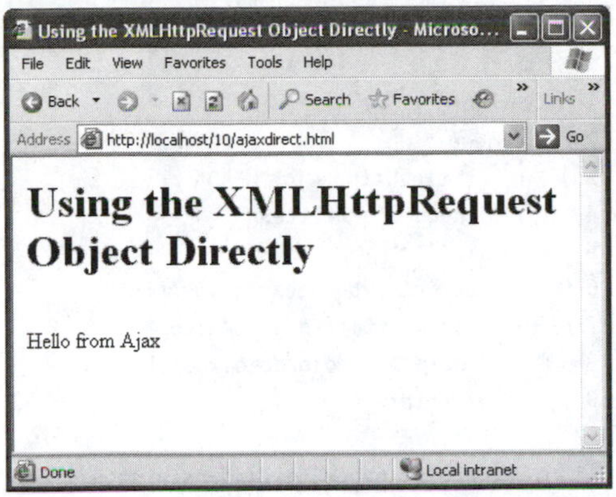

Figure 10.6 Using XMLHttpRequest to access the text downloaded by Ajax.

5. Save ajaxdirect.html.

6. Navigate to ajaxdirect.html in a browser. This example downloads and displays the data in data.txt (**Figure 10.6**).

✔ Tip

■ Do you want to download XML instead of plain text? Use the `responseXml` property instead of `responseText`.

Getting Header Data

You can access HTTP HEAD (or header) data to obtain information about the data you download with Ajax. For example, the HTTP "Last-Modified" header tells you when a file was last modified (that is, how recent the file is).

The example ajaxhead.html reads the "Last-Modified" header of a file, data.txt, and displays the date that the file was last modified. To access that header, you use the XMLHttpRequest object's getResponseHeader method.

To get header data using Ajax:

1. Open your text editor and create a file named data.txt with the contents *Hello from Ajax*; store that file in a directory on a Web server.

2. Open your text editor and create ajaxhead.html; store this file in the same directory as data.txt on the Web server.

3. Call dojo.xhrGet, and with the url parameter specify the URL of the data to download ("data.txt"), with the handleAs parameter specify the data format as "text", and with the load parameter specify the anonymous function to call to display the downloaded data in the Web page.

4. Add code to the anonymous function to read and display the "Last-Modified" header.

   Script 10.7 shows how your page should look after you make the additions.

Script 10.7 Getting header data using Ajax.

```
1    <html>
2     <head>
3       <title>Using Ajax HEAD
4         Requests</title>
5
6       <script type="text/javascript"
7         src="http://o.aolcdn.com/
8         dojo/1.1/dojo/dojo.xd.js">
9       </script>
10
11      <script type="text/javascript">
12        dojo.addOnLoad(function() {
13        dojo.xhrGet({
14
15          url : "data.txt",
16
17          handleAs : "text",
18
19          load : function(response, args) {
20
21          dojo.byId("div").innerHTML =
22            "data.txt was last modified on "
23          + args.xhr.getResponseHeader(
24            "Last-Modified");
25
26          return response;
27          },
28          error : function(response, args)
29          {
30
31            dojo.byId("div").innerHTML =
32              "Ajax error";
33
34            return response;
35          }
36        });
37      });
38     </script>
39    </head>
40
41    <body>
42      <h1>Using Ajax HEAD Requests</h1>
43      <br>
44      <div id="div"></div>
45    </body>
46   </html>
```

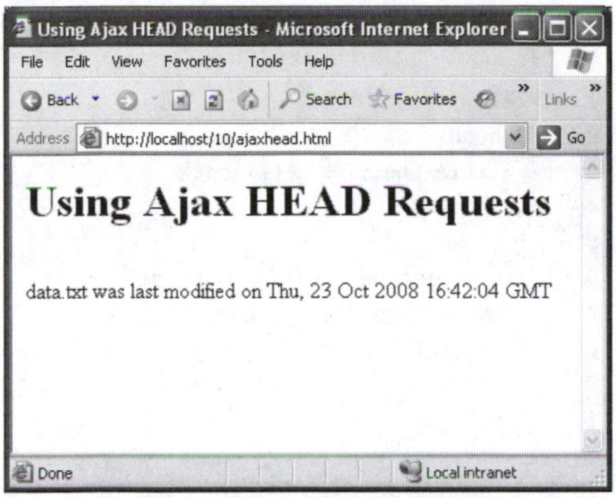

Figure 10.7 Getting the date that date.txt was last modified.

5. Save ajaxhead.html.

6. Navigate to ajaxhead.html in a browser. This example downloads and displays the data in data.txt (**Figure 10.7**).

✔ Tip

■ You can use the "`Content-Length`" header to determine the length of the response in bytes, and you can use the "`Content-Type`" header to get the MIME type of this content.

Creating Callback Chains

You can have Dojo call a number of callback functions in addition to the one you specify when calling xhrGet. The xhrGet function returns a Dojo object of type Deferred, and you can create chains of callback functions using the Deferred object.

Callback chains can be useful when you want to handle different Ajax-fetched data in different ways. For example, an XML record that should be displayed in an HTML table might be better sent to a different callback function than one that handles simple text. Using the addCallback method of the Deferred object, you can add appropriate callback functions depending on the Ajax operation the user has requested. You can also add error handlers to the Ajax operation with the addErrback method.

The example ajadeferred.html adds two callback functions, creating a callback chain.

To create a callback chain:

1. Open your text editor and create a file named data.txt with the contents *Hello from Ajax*; store that file in a directory on a Web server.

2. Open your text editor and create ajaxdeferred.html; store this file in the same directory as data.txt on the Web server.

3. Call dojo.xhrGet, and with the url parameter specify the URL of the data to download ("data.txt"), with the handleAs parameter specify the data format as "text", and with the load parameter specify the anonymous function to call to display the downloaded data in the Web page. Store the object returned by xhrGet in a variable named deferred.

Script 10.8 Creating a callback chain.

```
script
1   <html>
2     <head>
3       <title>Creating a Callback
4       Chain</title>
5
6       <script type="text/javascript"
7         src="http://o.aolcdn.com/
8         dojo/1.1/dojo/dojo.xd.js">
9       </script>
10
11      <script type="text/javascript">
12        dojo.addOnLoad(function() {
13
14          var deferred = dojo.xhrGet({
15            url: "data.txt",
16            timeout : 1000,
17            load : function(response, args) {
18              dojo.byId("div").innerHTML =
19              dojo.byId("div").innerHTML +
20              "Calling the callback chain...";
21
22              return response;
23            },
24            error : function(response, args)
25            {
26              return response;
27            }
28          });
29
30          deferred.addCallback(
31            function(result) {
32              dojo.byId("div").innerHTML =
33              dojo.byId("div").innerHTML +
34              "<br>Callback 1 got '" + result
35              + "'";
36
37              return result;
38            }
39          );
40
41          deferred.addCallback(
42            function (result) {
43              dojo.byId("div").innerHTML=
44              dojo.byId("div").innerHTML +
45              "<br>Callback 2 got '" + result
46              + "'";
47
48              return result;
```

(script continues)

Script 10.8 *continued*

```
                    script
49          }
50      );
51
52      deferred.addErrback(
53        function(result) {
54        dojo.byId("div").innerHTML=
55        dojo.byId("div").innerHTML +
56        "Error handler 1";
57
58        return result;
59        }
60      );
61
62      deferred.addErrback(
63        function(result) {
64        dojo.byId("div").innerHTML=
65        dojo.byId("div").innerHTML +
66        "Error handler 2";
67        return result;
68        }
69        );
70      });
71    </script>
72  </head>
73
74  <body>
75    <h1>Creating a Callback Chain</h1>
76    <div id="div"></div>
77  </body>
78  </html>
```

4. Add code to add two callback functions to the `Deferred` object using its `addCallback` method, and display the response sent to each callback function.

Script 10.8 shows how your page should look after you make the additions.

5. Save ajaxdeferred.html.

6. Navigate to ajaxdeferred.html in a browser. This example download the data in data.txt and passes it along the callback chain (**Figure 10.8**).

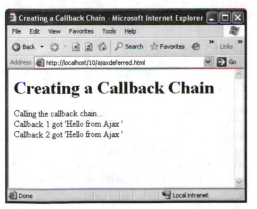

Figure 10.8 Using xhrGet to download data.

Canceling a Chained Request

You can cancel a callback chain with the Deferred object's cancel method. For instance, you may want to allow the user to cancel (say with a Cancel button) requests that are taking too long.

The example ajaxdeferredcancel.html creates a callback chain but then cancels the operation of that chain. As you'll see, the error handlers are called when a callback chain request is canceled.

To cancel a Deferred callback chain:

1. Open your text editor and create a file named data.txt with the contents *Hello from Ajax*; store that file in a directory on a Web server.

2. Open your text editor and create ajaxdeferredcancel.html; store this file in the same directory as data.txt on the Web server.

3. Call dojo.xhrGet, and with the url parameter specify the URL of the data you want to download ("data.txt"), with the handleAs parameter specify the data format as "text", and with the load parameter specify the anonymous function to call to display the downloaded data in the Web page. Store the object returned by xhrGet in a variable named deferred.

4. Add code to add two callback functions to the Deferred object using its addCallback method, and display the response sent to each callback function. In this example, cancel the callback chain with a call to the Deferred object's cancel method.

Script 10.9 Canceling a Deferred callback chain.

```
1   <html>
2     <head>
3     <title>Canceling a Callback
4       Chain</title>
5
6     <script type="text/javascript"
7       src="http://o.aolcdn.com/
8       dojo/1.1/dojo/dojo.xd.js">
9     </script>
10
11    <script type="text/javascript">
12      dojo.addOnLoad(function() {
13
14        var deferred = dojo.xhrGet({
15          url: "data.txt",
16          timeout : 1000,
17          load : function(response, args) {
18          dojo.byId("div").innerHTML =
19          dojo.byId("div").innerHTML +
20          "Calling the callback chain...";
21
22          deferred.cancel();
23
24          return response;
25          },
26          error : function(response, args)
27          {
28            return response;
29          }
30        });
31
32        deferred.addCallback(
33          function(result) {
34          dojo.byId("div").innerHTML =
35          dojo.byId("div").innerHTML +
36          "<br>Callback 1 got '" + result
37          + "'";
38
39          return result;
40          }
41        );
42
43        deferred.addCallback(
44          function (result) {
45          dojo.byId("div").innerHTML=
46          dojo.byId("div").innerHTML +
47          "<br>Callback 2 got '" + result
48          + "'";
49
```

(script continues)

Script 10.9 *continued*

```
50        return result;
51      }
52    );
53
54    deferred.addErrback(
55      function(result) {
56      dojo.byId("div").innerHTML =
57      dojo.byId("div").innerHTML +
58      "<br>Error handler 1 says:
59      operation was canceled";
60      return result;
61      }
62    );
63
64    deferred.addErrback(
65      function(result) {
66      dojo.byId("div").innerHTML =
67      dojo.byId("div").innerHTML +
68      "<br>Error handler 2 says:
69      operation was canceled";
70      return result;
71      }
72    );
73    });
74    </script>
75  </head>
76
77  <body>
78    <h1>Canceling a Callback Chain</h1>
79    <div id="div"></div>
80  </body>
81  </html>
```

5. Add code to add two `Errback` functions to the `Deferred` object using its `addErrback` method, and in their code, display a message indicating that the Ajax operation was canceled.

   Script 10.9 shows how your page should look after you make the additions.

5. Save ajaxdeferredcancel.html.

6. Navigate to ajaxdeferredcancel.html in a browser. This example downloads the data in data.txt, but it then cancels the callback chain and indicates that cancellation with messages from the error handlers (**Figure 10.9**).

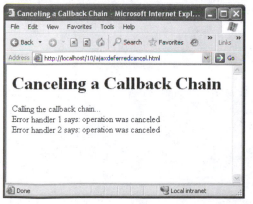

Figure 10.9 Canceling a callback chain and calling the error handlers.

Index

A

accordion containers, 55, 72–73
Ajax (Asynchronous JavaScript and XML), ix, 155
   accessing `XMLHttpRequest` object, 184–185
   callback chains
      canceling Deferred callback chain, 190–191
      creating, 188–189
   displaying error messages, 176–177
   Dojo overview, 2
   finishing operations, 178–179
   getting header data, 186–187
   implementing without Dojo, 156–157
   sending data using `POST` method, 170–171
   setting timeouts, 174–175
   synchronous operations, 182–183
   turn off browser caching, 180–181
   `xhrGet` method
      downloading XML, 160–161
      error handling, 164–165
      fetching JSON data, 162–163
      sending Ajax data, 166–167
      sending form data, 168–169
      using Ajax with Dojo, 158–159
animation, 135
   blending colors, 152–153
   controlling expansion speed, 146–147
   drag and drop operations, 148–149
   expanding elements, 144–145
   fades
      controlling speed, 138–139
      making elements fade out, 136–137
   sliding elements, 140–141
   toggling between visible and invisible elements, 150–151
   wiping elements, 142–143
AOL Content Delivery Network (CDN), acquiring Dojo, 5

application Dijits, 75, 95
   ColorPalette
      color picker dialog box, 88–89
      creating, 86–87
   Dialog
      accepting input in dialog box, 82–83
      creating, 80–81
   InlineEditBox, 108–109
   menus
      context, 98–99
      creating, 96–97
      pop-up, 100–101
      separators, 104–105
      traditional, 102–103
   ProgressBar, 84–85
   TitlePane, 106–107
   Toolbar
      adding images to toolbar, 92–93
      creating, 90–91
   Tooltip
      creating, 76–77
      using with images, 78–79
   Tree
      creating, 112–113
      creating data, 110–111
Asynchronous JavaScript and XML. *See* Ajax

B

`blendColors` method, 152–153
blending colors, 152–153
BorderContainer Dijits
   arranging around content pane, 60–61
   creating in code, 62–63
browsers, turn off caching, 180–181
`Button` module, 11
buttons
   adding radio buttons, 40–41
   combo buttons, adding, 52–53

buttons *(continued)*
  connecting to text box, 14–15
  creating, 11
  drop-down, adding, 50–51

C

caching, preventing with Ajax, 180–181
calendars, user selecting dates, 30–31
callback chains
  canceling Deferred callback chain, 190–191
  creating, 188–189
case sensitivity, Dijit event names, 15
check boxes, adding, 38–39
ColorPalette Dijits
  color picker dialog box, 88–89
  creating, 86–87
colors
  blending, 152–153
  ColorPalette Dijit
    color picker dialog box, 88–89
    creating, 86–87
combo boxes, adding, 42–43
combo buttons, adding, 52–53
constrained dragging, 128–129
containers
  accordion, 55, 72–73
  border
    arranging around content pane, 60–61
    creating in code, 62–63
  stack
    adding, 64–65
    creating in code, 66–67
  tab
    adding, 68–69
    creating in code, 70–71
ContentPane Dijits
  adding Dijits to, 58–59
  creating, 56–57
context menus, 98–99
CurrencyTextBox, 12

D

dates, user selecting from clickable calendar, 30–31
DateTextBox, 30–31
DateTimeTextBox, 12
debugging Dojo, 24–25
Dialog Dijits, 75
  accepting input in dialog box, 82–83
  creating, 80–81
`dijit.button` module, 11
Dijits, 2
  adding to moveables, 120–121
  application, 75, 95
    ColorPalette, 86–89
    Dialog, 80–83

InlineEditBox, 108–109
    menus, 96–105
    ProgressBar, 84–85
    TitlePane, 106–107
    Toolbar, 90–93
    Tooltip, 76–79
    Tree, 110–113
  buttons, creating, 11
  check boxes, adding, 38–39
  combo boxes, adding, 42–43
  combo buttons, adding, 52–53
  connecting to Dojo, 10
  DateTextBox, 30–31
  debugging Dojo, 24–25
  drop-down buttons, adding, 50–51
  JavaScript
    connecting to using `<script>` elements, 20–21
    creating in, 18–19
  layout, 55
    accordion containers, 72–73
    border containers, 60–63
    content pane, 56–59
    stack containers, 64–67
    tab containers, 68–71
  multiselect selection controls, adding, 46–47
  NumberSpinner, 34–35
  NumberTextBox, 28–29
  radio buttons, adding, 40–41
  sending data to Web sites, 22–23
  sliders, adding, 48–49
  text boxes, adding, 12
  TimeTextBox, 32–33
  toggle buttons, adding, 44–45
  ValidationTextBox, 26–27
`djconfig` attribute, 10, 24
Dojo
  acquiring from AOL CDN, 5
  installing, 3–4
  overview, 2
  tour, 6
    connecting button to text box, 14–15
    creating Web page, 7
    Dijits, 10–13
    running textbox.html, 16
    styles, 8–9
  Web site, 3
Dojo Extensions. *See* Dojox
dojo-release-x.y.z folders, 3
`dojo.addOnLoad` function, 13
`dojo.animateProperty` method, 144–145
`dojo.connect` method
  connecting button to text box, 14–15
  handing Dijit events, 13
`dojo.dnd.Source`
  dragging HTML elements, 130–131
  event handling, 132–133

`dojo.fadeIn` method, 137
`dojo.fadeOut` method, 136–137
`dojo.fx.slideTo` method, 140–141
`dojo.fx.wipeOut` method, 142–143
dojo.js files
    acquiring from AOL CDN, 5
    installing Dojo, 3–4
`dojo.require` statement, 10
`dojoType` attribute, 11
Dojox (Dojo Extensions), 2
downloads, Dojo, 3
drag motion, limiting, 128–129
dragging and dropping, 115
    creating draggable handles, 122–123
    `dojo.dnd.Source`
        dragging HTML elements, 130–131
        event handling, 132–133
    limiting drag motion, 128–129
    moveables
        adding Dijits, 120–121
        creating, 116–117
        using code to create, 118–119
        using multiple, 126–127
    responding to drag events, 124–125
drop-down buttons, adding, 50–51

E

easing functions, controlling fade speed, 138–139
elements
    animation, 135
        blending colors, 152–153
        controlling expansion speed, 146–147
        drag-and-drop operations, 148–149
        expanding elements, 144–145
        fades, 136–139
        sliding elements, 140–141
        toggling between visible and invisible elements, 150–151
        wiping elements, 142–143
    buttons
        adding radio buttons, 40–41
        combo buttons, adding, 52–53
        connecting to text box, 14–15
        creating, 11
        drop-down, adding, 50–51
    check boxes, adding, 38–39
    combo boxes, adding, 42–43
    Dijits. *See* Dijits
    images
        adding to toolbars, 92–93
        using with Tooltip Dijits, 78–79
    menus, 95
        context, 98–99
        creating, 96–97
        pop-up, 100–101

    separators, 104–105
    traditional, 102–103
sliders, adding, 48–49
text boxes
    creating, 12
    displaying text after button click, 14–15
    NumberSpinner, 34–35
    NumberTextBox, 28–29
    TimeTextBox, 32–33
    ValidationTextBox, 26–27
errors
    displaying Ajax errors, 176–177
    `xhrGet` method, 164–165
events
    dragging events, 132–133
    handling Dijit events, 13
expanding elements, 144–147

F–G

fades
    controlling speed, 138–139
    making elements fade out, 136–137
form Dijits. *See* Dijits

`getDisplayedValue` method, 30, 32
`getValue` method, 30, 32

H–I

headers, getting data with Ajax, 186–187
horizontal sliders, 49
HTML elements
    dragging, 130–131
    sending form data using Ajax, 168–169

images
    adding to toolbars, 92–93
    using with Tooltip Dijits, 78–79
inline edit boxes, 95
InlineEditBox Dijits, 108–109
installation, Dojo, 3–4
`invalidMessage` attribute, 28–29
invisible elements, 150–151
ISPs (Internet Service Providers), uploading files to, 4

J–K

JavaScript
    connecting to Dijits using `<script>` elements, 20–21
    creating Dijits, 18–19
    debugging Dojo, 24–25
    fetching JSON data with Ajax, 162–163
    ValidationTextBox, 26–27
JSON data, fetching with Ajax, 162–163

L

layout Dijits, 55
   accordion containers, 72–73
   border containers
      arranging around content pane, 60–61
      creating in code, 62–63
   content pane
      adding Dijits to, 58–59
      creating, 56–57
   stack containers
      adding, 64–65
      creating in code, 66–67
   tab containers
      adding, 68–69
      creating in code, 70–71
limiting drag motion, 128–129

M

menus, 95
   context, 98–99
   creating, 96–97
   pop-up, 100–101
   separators, 104–105
   traditional, 102–103
modules, 10
moveables
   adding Dijits, 120–121
   creating, 116–117
   using code to create, 118–119
   using multiple, 126–127
multiselect selection controls, adding, 46–47

N

Nihilo style theme, 8
numbers, user selecting with number spinner, 34–35
NumberSpinner, 12, 34–35
NumberTextBox, 12, 28–29
numeric validation, 28–29

O–P

parsing, 10
pop-up menus, 100–101
POST method, sending Ajax data, 170–171
ProgressBar Dijits, 84–85
promptMessage attribute, 28–29

R–S

radio buttons, adding, 40–41
RangeBoundTextBox, 12

<script> elements, connecting code to Dijits, 20–21
scripts
   accessing XMLHttpRequest object, 184–185
   accordion containers, 72–73
   adding check boxes, 38–39
   adding combo boxes, 42–43
   adding Dijits to moveables, 120–121
   adding radio buttons, 40–41
   adding text box Dijit, 12
   adding toggle buttons, 44–45
   Ajax timeouts, 174–175
   animation with drag-and-drop operations, 148–149
   blending colors, 152–153
   border containers, 60–63
   canceling Deferred callback chain, 190–191
   ColorPalette Dijits, 86–89
   combo buttons, 52–53
   connecting Dijits to Dojo, 10
   content pane, 56–59
   controlling fade speed, 138–139
   creating callback chains with Ajax, 188–189
   creating Dijits in code, 18–19
   creating Dojo button, 11
   creating Dojo Web page, 7
   creating moveables, 116–117
   debugging Dojo, 24–25
   Dialog Dijits, 80–83
   displaying Ajax errors, 176–177
   Dojo themes, 8–9
   downloading XML with Ajax, 160–161
   draggable hands, 122–123
   dragging HTML elements, 130–131
   drop-down buttons, 50–51
   error handling xhrGet method, 164–165
   expanding elements, 144–147
   fetching JSON data with Ajax, 162–163
   finishing Ajax operations, 178–179
   getting header data using Ajax, 186–187
   handling Dijit events, 13
   handling dragging events, 132–133
   implementing Ajax without Dojo, 156–157
   JavaScript connecting to Dijits, 20–21
   limiting drag motion, 128–129
   making elements fade out, 136–137
   moveables created with code, 118–119
   multiple moveables, 126–127
   multiselect selection controls, 46–47
   number validation, 28–29
   placing text in text box, 15
   ProgressBar Dijits, 84–85
   responding to drag events, 124–125
   sending Ajax data using POST method, 170–171
   sending Ajax data using xhrGet method, 166–167
   sending data to Web sites, 22–23
   sliders, 48–49

sliding elements, 140–141
stack containers, 64–67
synchronous Ajax operations, 182–183
tab containers, 68–71
togging between visible and invisible elements, 150–151
Toolbar Dijits, 90–93
Tooltip Dijits, 76–79
Tree Dijits, 110–113
turn off browser caching, 180–181
turning on validation, 26–27
user selecting from clickable calendar, 30–31
user selecting numbers with number spinner, 34–35
user selecting time from clickable control, 32–33
wiping elements, 142–143
separators, menus, 104–105
setValue method, 15
sliders, adding, 48–49
sliding elements, 140–141
Soria style theme, 8
special effects, 135
    blending colors, 152–153
    controlling expansion speed, 146–147
    drag-and-drop operations, 148–149
    expanding elements, 144–145
    fades
        controlling speed, 138–139
        making elements fade out, 136–137
    sliding elements, 140–141
    toggling between visible and invisible elements, 150–151
    wiping elements, 142–143
stack containers, 55
    adding, 64–65
    creating in code, 66–67
styles, 8–9

T

tab containers, 55
    adding, 68–69
    creating in code, 70–71
text
    displaying in text box, 14–15
    InlineEditBox Dijits, 108–109
text boxes
    creating, 12
    displaying text after button click, 14–15
    NumberSpinner, 34–35

NumberTextBox, 28–29
TimeTextBox, 32–33
ValidationTextBox, 26–27
textbox.html, running in browser, 16
themes, 8–9
time, user selecting from clickable control, 32–33
timeouts (Ajax), setting, 174–175
TimeTextBox, 32–33
title panes, 95
TitlePane Dijits, 106–107
toggle buttons, adding, 44–45
Toolbar Dijits, adding images to toolbar, 92–93
Tooltip Dijits, 75
    creating, 76–77
    using with images, 78–79
traditional menus, 102–103
Tree Dijits, 95
    creating, 112–113
    data file, 110–111
Tundra style theme, 8–9

U–V

Util package, 2

validation
    numeric validation, 28–29
    ValidationTextBox, 26–27
ValidationTextBox, 12, 26–27
vertical sliders, 49
visible elements, 150–151

W

Web page, creating, 7
widgets, 2
wiping elements, 142–143

X–Y–Z

XHMLHttpRequest object, 155
xhrGet method
    downloading XML with Ajax, 160–161
    error handling, 164–165
    fetching JSON data, 162–163
    sending Ajax data, 166–167
    sending form data, 168–169
    using Ajax with Dojo, 158–159
XML, downloading with Ajax, 160–161
XMLHttpRequest object, accessing directly, 184–185